ANIMALS IN RESEARCH
ISSUES AND CONFLICTS

ANIMALS
in
RESEARCH
Issues and Conflicts

J.J.McCoy

An Impact Book
Franklin Watts
New York   Chicago   London   Toronto   Sydney

Library of Congress Cataloging-in-Publication Data

McCoy, J. J. (Joseph J.), 1917–
  Animals in research : issues and conflicts / by J. J. McCoy.
     p.   cm.—(An Impact book)
  Includes bibliographical references and index.
  Summary: Examines the role of animals in testing for biological
research, medical purposes, and consumer products, and discusses
controversies raised over such practices.
  ISBN 0-531-13023-1
  1. Animal experimentation—United States.   2. Animal
experimentation—Canada.   3. Animal rights movement—United States.
4. Animal rights movement—Canada.   [1. Animal experimentation.
2. Animals—Treatment.]   I. Title.
HV4930.M35   1993
179′.4—dc20   92-21117 CIP AC

CONTENTS

INTRODUCTION

Animals and human beings have had a close relationship since prehistoric times. For the most part, it has been an association of symbiosis, with human beings receiving the lion's share of the benefits. It has also been a relationship in which animals have been exploited in various ways. None has engendered more emotion, censorship, and condemnation than the use of animals for experimentation.

Most of us accept the need to conduct research beneficial to human beings and animals. The conquest of human and animal diseases and the search for cures or treatments for others have involved the use of many animals of various species. The development of chemicals, food additives, pesticides, and other potentially harmful substances has also involved the use of many animals to test the safety of these substances.

But this use of animals is not without its opponents, some of whom have resorted to acts of violence and even terrorism. The opposition to the use of animals for experimentation is not new. Nineteenth-century English

7

humanitarians, such as Richard Martin and Jeremy Bentham, led the opposition to animal experimentation and cruelty to animals in general. However, their crusade against the inhumane treatment and torture of animals was a passive one, as were the efforts of early twentieth-century humanitarians in America. It is a different story today. A new breed of animal protectionists has emerged. They are members of what is called the animal rights movement. They believe in and pursue an active approach to eliminating cruelty to animals, especially in research laboratories.

The older and traditional humane societies or animal welfare groups asked people to be kind to animals and to refrain from cruel acts. They circulated articles, handbills, leaflets, and other literature aimed at reducing cruelty to animals. And they have operated animal shelters for stray or unwanted animals.

Not so with the animal rights groups. They are more militant, more direct, and more aggressive in their campaign to free animals from exploitation. Their demands range from the reduction of the number of animals used in research to the wider use of alternatives to the total abolition of any form of animal exploitation. In backing up these demands, the animal rights advocates have resorted to demonstrations, boycotts, corporate shareholder resolutions, laboratory break-ins, theft of animals, destruction of equipment, violence, and even threats of bodily harm or death to researchers.

The growing strength of the animal rights groups and their well-filled treasuries are a matter of concern to the scientific community. So is the influence that animal rights activists have with the public and even with some politicians. Researchers have been put on the defensive and have been compelled to justify their studies and experiments. This they have done, but mainly to opponents who have only one objective in mind: the elimination of animal research and consumer product testing. Researchers have not only had to justify their research but to defend their laboratories and research facilities against vandalism.

Why has the use of animals in research and testing become a national issue, second, perhaps, only to the human abortion issue? What is there about dogs, cats, monkeys and other primates, guinea pigs, hamsters, rabbits, mice, and rats that evokes such emotional and violent response when they are used in research? What are the issues in this controversy, a controversy that has economic, ethical, moral, political, and social consequences?

The issue is of national importance because many Americans and Canadians feel deeply about it. Many do not believe we have the right to subject animals to pain and suffering in the laboratories. Others have not made up their minds, while still others believe that benefits to humanity are worth the sacrifice of animals. It is a complex issue, one that has no pat answers. At the core of the issue is whether animals have rights, an old concept that dates to the Middle Ages (the period in European history from about A.D. 476 to A.D. 1453). For centuries the Judeo-Christian concept of the separateness of human beings and animals dominated the treatment of animals.

People were told that animals had no souls; therefore they had no rights. Most philosophers went along with this church dictum. René Descartes, the seventeenth-century French mathematician and philosopher, wrote that animals were nothing more than "cleverly built machines." As such, they had no feelings or conscious responses. No animal, according to Descartes, could be compared to a human in any way.

Most of the early biologists and zoologists were more concerned with the classification and natural history of animals than with any ethical or moral questions concerning their treatment. Few, if any, attempts were made to establish a relationship between human beings and animals.

But this thinking changed in the nineteenth century. Charles Darwin, the English naturalist, dispelled some of the earlier beliefs and dogma regarding a relationship between human beings and animals. In his monumental work, *On the Origin of Species by Means of Natural Selection* published in 1859, Darwin proposed that all animals evolved from more primitive forms by a process he called "natural selection." That is, nature selected the most vigorous and best-suited animal forms for survival. And eventually, these primitive forms became more complex.

Darwin did not discuss human beings in *On the Origin of Species*. However, in 1871, he published a study of human evolution, *The Descent of Man*, in which he set forth the theory that humans also evolved from primitive forms. Thus, if Darwin's theories were correct, people and animals were part of an entity, a whole natural system. And if this was true, then it followed that human beings and animals were related, that there was a direct link between them. This thought caused as much controversy and consternation in America as it did in Europe. It established a physical, if not a spiritual, relationship between people and animals.

Modern scientific thought supposes, despite some missing links, that there is no break in the long chain of animal forms that have evolved over time. Complex animals forms, such as human beings, have evolved from simpler forms. While human beings have some different characteristics and behavior patterns, the overall difference is one of the degree of complexity when humans are compared to other animals.

Many people cling to the old Judeo-Christian concept of humans' preeminence or superiority over animals. Many others, including animal rights advocates, do not accept this concept. They reject the idea that there is a "superior" species. Since there is no superior species, human beings do not have the right to mistreat animals or exploit them in any way, including using them in research.

Various species and large numbers of animals are used in biomedical and behavioral research, product testing, and education every year. But among many people, the experimental use of cats and dogs causes more anguish and provokes more condemnation than does the similar use of other animals. There are some valid reasons for this. For one thing, cats and dogs are very popular pets. Millions of them are kept in homes in the United States and Canada, not to mention elsewhere in the world. But more than that, cats and dogs have a special bond with human beings. In many households they are accorded equal status with their human owners, and are looked upon as members of the family.

The bond between these two animals and human beings goes back thousands of years: more than twenty thousand years in the case of the dog and about five thousand years for the cat. The pact between human and dog, a pact that has lasted a long time, began when wild dogs and the cave people joined forces. There are several theories as to how the cave dwellers and wild dogs formed a pact of mutualism. Konrad Lorenz, the Austrian psychologist and animal behaviorist, gives an interesting account of this ancient pact in his book *Man Meets Dog*. Both man and dog benefitted from this alliance. The dog served the cave people as a hunting companion, pet, and guardian. The cave people, in turn, fed the dog and protected him from larger predators such as the saber-toothed tiger and dire wolf.

The contributions of the dog to modern society need no listing or elaboration; the proof is in the facts. Dog ownership is at an all-time high according to the Pet Industry Advisory Council, a lobbying group based in Washington, D.C. In recent years, the influence of dogs (and other pets) on the mental and physical health of human beings has been documented in numerous articles, papers, and reports. But it is the loyalty, devotion, and companionship of this unique animal that make it difficult for people to accept its use in biomedical research.

What records we have of the cat's early association with human beings are from ancient Egyptian tombs and mastabas (*mastabas* are rectangular structures with sloping sides and flat roofs; many of them contained paintings and likenesses of human beings and cats). Judging by the evidence found in these structures, cats were held in high esteem by the ancient Egyptians.

In fact, cats were even regarded as minor gods. Some Egyptian deities were supposed to have catlike features and traits. For example, Ra, the sun god, was closely identified with the male cat. Bast or Pasht, the cat goddess, was a very popular deity. Her popularity is substantiated by the large number of her images, ranging from life-size paintings to tiny cat earrings found in Egyptian tombs.

Cats became popular pets and rodent catchers in other countries. Herodotus, the fifth century B.C. historian and traveler, extolled the virtues and characteristics of Egyptian cats in Book II of his *Histories*. Eventually, the reputation of the cat as a pet and rodent hunter grew and this diminutive feline was in great demand. It soon became a popular pet in all parts of the world. Today, cats occupy a special niche in our society. While they differ from dogs in temperament and their attitudes toward people (some people say that cats are more selective in their association with human beings), most cats have a close relationship with their owners. This unique and interesting animal is also used in various types of experiments, the victim or subject of biomedical and behavioral research, depending on viewpoint.

The other animals commonly used in research—rabbits, hamsters, guinea pigs, mice, rats, monkeys, and other nonhuman primates—have lesser or no special bonds with human beings. Nevertheless, many people deplore their use in research. These animals, along with the dog and cat, are the protagonists, the principal figures, in the animals in research controversy.

This book is a synthesis of that controversy. It is an effort to present a balanced view or provide "both sides of the story," examining the main issues and conflicts of that controversy.

WHY USE ANIMALS IN RESEARCH?

The use of animals for experimentation dates back to ancient times, when Greek and Roman philosophers and physicians explored the bodies of animals to learn more about anatomy and physiology. Galen, the Greek anatomist and physician, is credited with being the founder of experimental physiology. His studies were conducted on a variety of animals. Pliny the Elder, the Roman scholar; Andreas Vesalius, the Flemish physician; and Aristotle, the noted Greek philosopher, sated their curiosity about the workings of the animal body by studying the anatomy and physiology of different animals.

These early animal experiments were crude by the standards of modern biomedical research. Little was known about the mechanisms of the human and animal body. Aristotle, for example, believed the heart was the center of the nervous system. He is said to have experimented on as many as fifty species of animals in studies of the nervous and circulatory systems. In ancient Constantinople (now Istanbul, Turkey), Flavius Vegetius Renatus, a Roman physician, was a pioneer in the study of the animal digestive, circulatory, respiratory, nervous, and genitourinary systems. Vegetius, as he was known in ancient times, advocated careful surgical techniques when experimenting on animals.

Among the old civilizations, that of the Hindus came closest to having what might be called a systematic practice of animal or veterinary medicine. In this practice, various animals were dissected in efforts to learn about animal anatomy and physiology. Despite the experimenting on animals, the Hindus regarded all living creatures as brothers.

Scholars who have translated some of the ancient Sanskrit veterinary writings tell of special hospitals for animals operated by the Hindu state. Here, Hindu animal doctors studied and treated the diseases of animals. Among the animals listed in the Sanskrit writings were elephants, horses, cattle, poultry, and various cage birds.

The Hindu doctors had enough knowledge of animal anatomy to establish a system of animal medicine. They performed minor surgery, cauterized wounds (by burning or searing them), set broken bones, and resorted to bloodletting when all other methods failed. The Sanskrit writings also mention that Hindu animal doctors practiced obstetrics, taking special care of pregnant cattle and elephants.

In other ancient cultures, such as the Babylonian, Hebrew, and Arab, animal medicine and experimentation were closely linked with human medicine. Superstition, ritual, and magic were rampant. Anyone professing to know something about animals could set himself up as an animal doctor. Consequently, the field of animal medicine was staffed by farriers (horseshoers), livestock farmers, and stablemen.

After hundreds of years of quasi-scientific animal and human medical practices, true scientific thought emerged in Europe. Roger Bacon, the thirteenth-century English philosopher, proposed a system of natural history that was far superior to anything before. He called for new scientific experimentation, criticizing long-accepted theories and practices.

However, clerical opposition to scientific thought and experimentation, especially in the field of medicine, was very strong. Human and animal experimentation was taboo. The clergy believed that human and animal diseases were concrete evidence of divine wrath. Scientists and scholars had no right to interfere with these visitations, since that responsibility belonged to the church.

This position of the clergy was especially troublesome to physicians, for they were forbidden to dissect human cadavers. Physicians, artists, and sculptors wishing to study the anatomy of the human body or dissect it had to steal cadavers and work on them in secret, risking discovery and punishment by death. As a result of the restrictions on the use of human corpses, physicians turned to the use of animals to learn more about disease and its effects on the animal body.

Today, animals are used in research for a number of reasons, chief among them being the restriction, for ethical and moral reasons, on the use of human beings as research subjects. In 1964, the World Medical Association (WMA) stated at its international conference in Helsinki, Finland, "Clinical research must conform to the moral and scientific principles that justify medical research." The WMA statement emphasized the fact that "medical research should be based on laboratory and animal experiments or other scientifically established facts." This policy was, in effect, a repudiation of the medical and behavioral experiments performed on human beings by Nazi physicians and scientists during World War II.

Although there is some research and experimentation carried out on human beings today (psychiatric and psychological studies, drug therapy, and the like), animals form the bulk of biomedical research subjects. The National Academy of Sciences Natural Resource Council (NRC) spent three years studying the issue of the use of animals in research. In its assessment, the NRC stated that "animals are a critical part of human health care." Also cited in the report was a long list of medical advances and achievements due to the use of animals in research. The NRC committee that undertook the study admitted that laboratory animals have been mistreated by some members of the scientific community. However, they added that it was not to be supposed that abuse or neglect of laboratory animals was widespread.[1]

Which animals and how many of them are used annually in biomedical research? Laboratory animals include cats, dogs, rabbits, guinea pigs, hamsters, mice, rats, monkeys, and nonhuman primates such as chimpanzees, and, in the agricultural field, horses, cattle, sheep, goats, and swine. As for how many animals are used each year, estimates vary according to the source. Estimates in animal rights literature range from 20 to 70 million. However, the Office of Technology Assessment gives a figure of 17 to 22 million, of which 90 percent are rodents. The percentage of cats and dogs, according to this assessment, is 1 to 2 percent, or about 200,000 of these animals.[2]

The use of animals to test the safety of consumer products such as cosmetics, drugs, and food might be called a form of research. Mice, rats, and rabbits are commonly used for product testing, but other animals may be, depending on the particular test. Estimates on the number of animals used in product testing vary and range from several million to half of all the animals used in research. The number of animals used in education is smaller, somewhere in the area of 50,000 to 60,000 animals in use in medical and veterinary schools. (There are no figures for animals used in secondary education.)

THE VALUE OF ANIMALS
AS RESEARCH TOOLS _____

In general, animals are used in research to study living systems. Animals, with the exception of elephants, turtles and tortoises, and a few other species, have relatively short lives. For example, mice have a life span of about three years. The relatively short life span of laboratory animals enables researchers to conduct certain studies and experiments that would not be possible on human beings because of the longer life span of humans.

Some animal diseases are identical to or are closely related to human diseases, for example, rabies, tuberculosis, leptospirosis (infectious jaundice), and anthrax (a bacterial disease affecting animals and human beings). Animals susceptible to these diseases can be used as models for studying the disease.

Researchers use animals to learn more about common animal and human disorders. Animals contribute to the growing fund of knowledge about genetics, psychology, and neurology. They are proving valuable in their contributions to the fields of mental illness, drug addiction, and senility. On the other hand, these advances and achievements have caused pain and suffering to millions of animals, a fact that cannot be denied.

Opponents of biomedical research argue that the findings from animal research cannot be extrapolated to human beings. While this may be regarded more as an opinion than as a fact, it is circulated by antivivisectionists in their newsletters, pamphlets, and other literature. *Vivisection* is the act of cutting into or dissecting the body of a living animal, especially for the purpose of research. The word is derived from the Latin *vivas*, meaning alive, and *sectio*, the act of cutting. *Antivivisectionist*, then, is a broadened term that means anyone opposed to any form of experimentation on live animals.

It is true that some findings from animal experiments or tests may not be applicable to human beings. But there are enough similarities between human beings and animals to justify animal research. Dr. Maud Slye, an early twentieth-century cancer researcher, conducted studies on mice. Her studies involved spontaneous tumors in mice. Lung and other tumors that developed in her mice did so naturally; they were not implanted or otherwise artificially produced.

Dr. Slye's studies investigated the possibility that cancer could be inherited. One of her conclusions, based on the growth of spontaneous tumors in her mice, as well as autopsies performed on several thousand mice, was that a recessive gene was responsible for the inheritance of cancer. When she stated that her findings could be extrapolated to human beings, critics said she was wrong. Dr. Slye's response was "tissue is tissue." It must be added that Dr. Slye's recessive gene conclusion was also challenged. (She was conducting cancer research in the early 1930s, before the discovery of deoxyribonucleic acid [DNA], when her conclusion that cancer was caused by a recessive gene was disputed.) Dr. Slye was not quite right, but we know today that heredity does play a role in some forms of cancer. This explains why physicians taking a patient's history ask whether anyone in the family has had cancer.

Similarities between animals and human beings do exist. For instance, there is a biochemical connection between animals and human beings, an example being the serum albumin found in the blood of human beings and all other vertebrates. Hemoglobin is produced in all mammals, including human beings, and researchers have demonstrated that the hemoglobin of chimpanzees is identical to that of human beings. It has also been learned that there is some degree of similarity between the DNA (deoxyribonucleic acid, the hereditary material of organisms) recombination of human beings and that of animals.

20

Mice, hamsters, and guinea pigs have some physiological responses similar to those seen in human beings. And it is well known that cats, dogs, and other animals can be infected with certain human diseases, and vice versa.

Ethologists, or animal behaviorists, have pointed out that some animals have altruistic behavior similar to that of human beings. For example, dogs, cats, and nonhuman primates practice behavior patterns that indicate these animals care for each other. And wolves, baboons, chimpanzees, orangutans, and gorillas have social tendencies similar to those of human beings.

Many of the new insights and discoveries about human behavior have resulted from basic studies on animals. Since it is not always feasible to test new ideas or concepts about behavior on human beings, some animals have served as substitutes or surrogates. While certain animals are ideal for such research, there are some limitations. John Paul Scott, an American zoologist and ethologist, points out that "both the behavior of the experimental animal and the corresponding human activity must be so well known that we can be certain we are working with identical phenomena."[3]

There are dissimilarities, too. These can have a bearing on the value of using certain animals for biomedical research or product testing. For example, animals may have different responses to drugs or chemicals. A case in point is thalidomide, a sedative given to European women in the 1960s to prevent miscarriages. However, thalidomide turned out to be a chemical that resulted in thousands of deformed children. Yet the drug did not produce deformed young in the animals on which it was originally tested. Other dissimilarities involve the posture of animals versus that of human beings, the reasoning power of human beings, the special capacities of both animals and human beings, and the differences in characteristics and traits.

Are the similarities and dissimilarities the only basis

for judging whether animals can be used for research? Animal rights advocates say they are not, that there are also ethical and moral considerations. Some of them refer to the beliefs of Jeremy Bentham, the nineteenth-century English philosopher and humanitarian mentioned earlier. Bentham believed that all moral, social, or political action should be directed toward achieving the greatest good for the greatest number of people. He argued that only an animal's capacities to suffer or experience pleasure are morally relevant. He stated that the issue of animal welfare was not whether animals could "reason or talk, but can they suffer?" Other animal welfare advocates have stronger feelings and beliefs about the use of animals in research; their opposition is discussed in Chapter Six.

Various federal government agencies and departments use animals for biomedical research and product testing. The U.S. Department of Health and Human Services conducts such studies in four of its divisions: National Institutes of Health (NIH), Food and Drug Administration (FDA), National Institute on Drug Abuse (NIDA), and National Institute for Occupational Safety and Health (NIOSH). NIH is the largest of these agencies and uses many more animals than the other federal agencies. Other agencies or departments that use animals for research are the U.S. Department of the Interior, Department of Transportation, Consumer Product Safety Commission (CPSC), Environmental Protection Agency (EPA), National Aeronautics and Space Administration (NASA), and the Veterans Administration.

Animals are also used in experiments conducted by researchers in colleges and universities. They are also used in large numbers by manufacturers testing the safety of products such as cosmetics, chemicals, and pharmaceuticals. Some of the federal agencies, such as the FDA, EPA, CPSC, and NIOSH, often specify the use of animals in testing consumer products.

Animal rights advocates and antivivisectionists challenge the use of animals in research, arguing that besides being inhumane, it is unnecessary. In addition, they claim that laboratory animals are abused.

There are some notable examples in which opponents charged that animals were misused in research. One of these was a study known as the "maternal and sibling deprivation studies," conducted by Harvey Harlow and associates at the University of Wisconsin in the early 1960s. This research is still referred to by animal rights advocates and antivivisectionists as an example of cruelty to and misuse of animals in research.

In the Harlow study, infant rhesus monkeys were separated from their mothers shortly after birth and kept in isolation. However, they were given surrogate mothers. Some of the baby monkeys were given heated cloth dolls, while others were given nothing more than wire mesh structures. Some of the baby monkeys were isolated for three or four months, while others remained in isolation for a year.

The monkeys isolated for only a few months were, after being taken out of isolation, able to relate to people and other monkeys and to get along with their peers. But the monkeys isolated for a year were unable to form any kind of bond and had very poor social interaction.

When the Harlow experiments were publicized, there was an outcry of protest from antivivisectionists and humanitarians. The study was denounced as inhumane, high in suffering and unwarranted stress. Harlow and his associates were condemned and vilified. The usefulness of the study was also criticized.

Some aspects of the study merited criticism. It is doubtful that this use of animals would be accepted today, considering the standards now in existence for the care and use of laboratory animals. For example, the isolation of monkeys and nonhuman primates is prohibited under the regulations of the Federal Animal Welfare Act.

Was this use of animals wrong? Inhumane? Was the study of little value, as some critics charged? Humanitarians said yes; most scientists said no. The Harlow experiments, stressful though they may have been, contributed to the advancement of knowledge in the field of pediatrics. They showed that attachments to a single mother figure are not necessary for normal social development. This is considered an important contribution to the field of human development.

Another research study that allegedly involved the misuse and mistreatment of animals occurred at the American Museum of Natural History in New York City in the summer of 1976. The research was concerned with the sexual responses of desensitized cats. It was conducted by Lester R. Aaronson and associates. Aaronson was chairman and curator of the museum's Department of Animal Behavior. His project was funded by the National Institutes of Health and the National Institute of Child Health and Human Development.

Cats were chosen for this study because they are relatively complex animals. Considerable data on their brains and nervous systems, showing some similarities between their brains and those of human beings, were available to the researchers. After some nerve surgery, the cats in the study became disoriented and lost interest in sexual activity.

Henry Spira, a former student of Peter Singer, a professor of ethics and the author of *Animal Liberation*, led the attack on Aaronson and the American Museum of Natural History. Aaronson was accused of being a "pervert and sadist." His study was labeled as worthless as far as any relevancy to human beings was concerned. The experiments were attacked as cruel and inhumane.

The main purpose of Aaronson's study was to gain knowledge about low and high sexual activity that could be applied to human beings, with some side benefits for cats. Aaronson's laboratory and procedures were repeatedly monitored by the National Society for Medical Research, National Institutes of Health, the Animal and Plant Health Inspection Service of the United States Department of Agriculture (APHIS), the American Society for the Prevention of Cruelty to Animals, and other animal welfare organizations. His experiments were conducted in conformity with the regulations in the Animal Welfare Act. Were Aaronson's studies relevant to human sexual activity? The Division of Research Grants, National Institutes of Health, thought so when it approved funding for the project. So did other scientific organizations. Nevertheless, the opposition to Aaronson's experiments was so strong that the museum eventually cancelled the project. However, there were those who thought that the charges against Aaronson's research were out of proportion to the discomfort suffered by the cats.

There are more examples of the use of animals in research and testing that have been condemned by animal rights advocates as unnecessary, cruel, or needlessly painful or stressful. Some of them are discussed in the chapters on biomedical research and consumer product testing.

Despite the charges of animal rights advocates, the use of animals in research is regulated by law and by guidelines. Various public and private organizations have designed procedures for the care and use of research animals. The New York Academy of Science, Committee on Animal Research, issued guidelines on the treatment and use of animals in biomedical research, consumer product testing, and educational studies or experiments. The American Diabetes Association (ADA) issued a policy statement on the use of animals in diabetes research. The ADA policy statement emphasizes the humane care of animals used in any research or educational program concerned with diabetes. The National Academy of Sciences, Psychologists for the Ethical Treatment of Animals, American Medical Association, Physicians Committee for

Responsible Medicine, Canadian Council on Animal Care, and other organizations have issued position papers or have drawn up guidelines regarding the care and use of laboratory animals.

There is always some risk of abuse or mistreatment in the use of animals for research. The very nature or purpose of some animal experiments dictates that pain and stress will occur. An important question to ask is, When does an experiment produce pain and suffering to a point where it is unacceptable in human terms? The question of who makes this decision also arises. It is also debatable whether the results of an experiment justify the pain and suffering it causes. However, it is necessary to remember that not every experiment will yield results beneficial to human beings or animals. And regardless of the expected results of an experiment, some pain, discomfort, or stress will probably be present.

Researchers are well aware that the condition and well-being of their laboratory animals are crucial factors in the yield and validity of their experiments. The responses of unhealthy or stressed animals can greatly affect the results of a study or experiment. Researchers know that undue pain or distress can produce unwanted variables in their findings; these variables can interfere with the interpretation of the results. Only a negligent researcher would mistreat his or her laboratory animals.

New technology may have a marked effect on the use of animals in research. The developing field of biotechnology is having a definite influence on the kinds and numbers of animals used in certain types of experiments. One way in which biotechnology is reducing the number of animals used in research is in the development of new tests that will be acceptable to regulatory agencies such as the FDA, EPA, and NIOSH.

But biotechnology may require the use of more animals of different species; it is still too soon to tell. At the present time, it is estimated that biotechnology uses about 11 percent of all laboratory rodents (mice, rats, guinea pigs, and hamsters); about 5 percent of the pigs; and close to 2 percent of the rabbits and dogs available for research. This new field of research, however, uses very few nonhuman primates or cats.

An example of biotechnology is research being conducted on the rabies virus. Early rabies research conducted by the nineteenth-century French chemist Louis Pasteur involved the search for a vaccine. The rabies virus is transmitted through the bite of a rabid animal, such as a dog, fox, or raccoon. Pasteur's experiments revealed that the rabies virus localized in the animal brain in the form of what are called Negri bodies. He cultured viruses from the brain tissue of rabid dogs and injected them into rabbits. In every case, rabies appeared in the rabbits in about fourteen days.

From these experiments, Pasteur went on to develop a rabies vaccine that protected dogs and other animals. Once the vaccine was effective on dogs, Pasteur set out to develop one for humans. After considerable experimenting that included human subjects, he perfected a system of inoculations that prevented the development of rabies in a patient bitten by a rabid dog. This system of inoculations became known as the Pasteur treatment for rabies. It was not a cure; there is no known cure for rabies.

New diagnostic tests are using antibodies produced in cell cultures. From these cultures, vaccines can be developed without the use of live animals. Advances in determining molecular structure can be used to predict biochemical functions. Here again, a reduction in the use of animals can result. Scientists can employ such advances to determine the active sites of molecules and even the locations of viruses. Data obtained from such experiments can be used in the development of synthetic drugs in a more direct way. However, new drugs or compounds will still have to undergo safety tests on animals, and animals will still be needed for the validation of results.

The use of animals for research and product testing remains an emotional issue. It has precipitated a confrontation between animal rights activists and responsible scientists that has far-reaching effects, especially on the health and welfare of the public. The position of some scientists that the interests and welfare of animals must be secondary to those of human beings fans the flames of the controversy. Inflammatory rhetoric from both sides clouds the issues, often misleading and confusing the public.

In the long run, it might be said that the use of animals in research is a matter for conscience and values. There are many questions to be answered. Are the lives of human beings more important than those of animals? Were the lives of the rhesus monkeys used by Dr. Jonas Salk in developing the Salk polio vaccine more important than those of the millions of children now spared this crippling disease? If pain or serious risk to human health or life arises, is it not better—not to mention more morally correct—to experiment on animals rather than on human beings?

Animals, then, are used as substitutes for human beings in a wide variety of experiments and studies. They have served as organisms on which toxic chemicals and other harmful substances are tested. And they are used by students to learn about the anatomy and physiology of the animal body. All of these uses are condemned by animal rights activists and antivivisectionists.

Biomedical and Behavioral Research

Various species of animals are used in biomedical and behavioral research. Scientists in these fields conduct or perform experiments in many disciplines—bacteriology, cardiology, endocrinology, nutrition, neurology, immunology, nephrology, oncology, pathology, virology, and psychology. The use of animals in these research areas has produced medical advances, discoveries, and new techniques that researchers say could not otherwise have been achieved or developed.

SOME MEDICAL ADVANCES AND ACHIEVEMENTS

While animals have added to the store of medical knowledge in past centuries, the greatest advances have occurred in the twentieth century. An important discovery in the early part of the century was the identification and development of insulin. This major medical breakthrough resulted from research on diabetes in dogs conducted

29

by the Canadian physician Frederick Banting and his associates. Although there were some treatments for diabetes at the time of Dr. Banting's research, none was effective.

Diabetes is marked by an insufficiency of insulin, which is manufactured in the pancreas. The pancreas is a long, thin gland situated crosswise behind the stomach. It has two functions: it produces enzymes to help digestion, and it produces insulin and glucagon.

Dr. Banting believed it possible to make an extract out of tissue from beef pancreas that could be used in the treatment of diabetes. In Banting's experiments, a number of dogs were used, some of which had undergone the removal of their pancreas. An extract of beef pancreas was eventually developed, and Banting called it "isletin." It was so named because the beef tissue used in making the extract came from that part of the pancreas known as the islets of Langerhans. This section of the pancreas was named after the nineteenth-century German pathologist Paul Langerhans. Later, the extract's name was changed to insulin, which is derived from the Latin word *insula*, or island.

Today, thousands of lives are saved every year by insulin. Children and adults with diabetes mellitus lead normal lives with injections or oral doses of insulin. Banting received world recognition for the research and development of insulin. He freely admitted that without his laboratory dogs he could not have produced it.

Another twentieth-century medical milestone was the development of a vaccine against poliomyelitis, a disease that cripples both children and adults. Dr. Jonas Salk, a microbiologist, developed the first polio vaccine in the 1950s. Salk's research was conducted on rhesus monkeys. Prior to the development of a vaccine, thousands of people, young and old alike, were stricken by the disease. Polio causes atrophy of the arms and legs, body paralysis, and in the more severe forms death, or life in an iron lung or respirator.

In more recent years, procedures for organ transplants were developed on dogs, nonhuman primates, and other animals. The transplantation of skin, cornea, and other organs could not, according to researchers, be made a safe procedure without the experience and knowledge gained from animal experiments.

Early in the development of human kidney transplantation procedures, surgeons faced a high rejection rate. Kidneys taken from an unrelated person and transplanted into another did not work. However, experiments on dogs using the drug 6-mercaptopurine (an immunosuppressant) after transplanting an organ prolonged the retention time of an organ from an unrelated animal.

The development of cyclosporin, an immunosuppressant used after human organ transplantations, proved to be a major advance in this field of medicine. After five years of testing on mice, rats, and other animals, cyclosporin was used in human trials. Since this immunosuppressant became available for use after heart transplantations, the survival rate of patients receiving new hearts dramatically increased.

Open-Heart Surgery

Open-heart surgery is no longer headline news. But in the 1970s, such surgery on human beings had to await the results of experiments performed on cats and dogs. These experiments involved the design and use of heart/lung machines vital to open-heart surgery. Researchers working on this project in the early 1930s clamped off dog and cat arteries and routed the animal's blood through the forerunner of the present-day heart/lung machine.

Later, the early heart/lung machine was improved upon by a roller pump developed by Dr. Michael DeBakey, an American specialist in heart surgery. The roller pump changed the course of the blood from the vasculature into and through the heart/lung machine. In doing so, it added oxygen to the blood. This pump, first developed and used on animals, is now an essential part of the modern heart/lung machine.

THE RHESUS FACTOR

The rhesus, or Rh, factor was identified during tests on rhesus monkeys. The Rh factor involves the presence of very complicated substances on the surface of human red blood cells. Experiments on the monkeys revealed two types of Rh factor: Rh positive and Rh negative.

Rhesus factor incompatibility between a woman and a fetus she is carrying causes problems. This incompatibility can be described as an antagonism between the rhesus blood groups of a mother and a developing baby. Rhesus incompatibility, as researchers learned from their experiments on monkeys, only occurs if the mother has Rh negative blood and the baby has Rh positive blood by way of Rh positive genes from the father. However, researchers also learned that an offspring may inherit Rh negative genes from a father with Rh positive blood. The Rh factor research on monkeys and its application to human beings were significant breakthroughs in the understanding of the immunology of pregnancy.

HEPATITIS

Hepatitis, or inflammation of the liver, is a debilitating viral disease. There are several types of hepatitis. In acute hepatitis A, the liver becomes tender and enlarged. Bilirubin, a substance produced when the liver breaks down old red blood cells, collects in the bloodstream and causes jaundice. The virus may be present for several weeks before any signs or symptoms appear. Acute hepatitis A is highly infectious and can be transmitted through contaminated blood or feces. There is no specific treatment for this form of hepatitis. However, bed rest and a nutritious diet help speed recovery.

Acute hepatitis B is also highly contagious. The symptoms are the same as those seen in acute hepatitis A. The main difference between the two types of hepatitis is the duration and severity of the symptoms, which include weakness, loss of appetite, and abdominal discomfort. The symptoms of acute hepatitis B are more severe and last longer than those of acute hepatitis A.

Dogs are susceptible to a form of hepatitis. Infectious canine hepatitis is spread by contact with nasal discharge or urine. (It is not caused by the same hepatitis viruses that infect human beings.) A vaccine against infectious canine hepatitis was developed about thirty years ago. It is only recently that a vaccine effective against acute hepatitis B has been developed.

BURNS

The treatment of burn victims is a major concern. Hundreds of people are severely burned each year. Some are scarred for life by burns caused by fire or chemicals. Third-degree burns are the most devastating, since all layers of the skin are destroyed by prolonged contact with heat, flame, or chemicals.

In 1944, a British biologist, P. B. Medawar, experimented with skin transplants on cattle. His subject was a cow known as a "free martin," a sexually maldeveloped female calf born as a twin to a bull calf. Male hormones transferred to the female calf through the placenta while she is still in the womb render the female calf sterile. The bull calf is not sterile.

Medawar's experiments showed that skin and other tissue could be successfully transplanted between the bull calf and his free martin twin at any stage of their lives. In short, they tolerated each other's tissue and antigens (proteins). Medawar's pioneering work with cattle in this important area of medicine led to other advances in the treatment of burns in animals and human beings.

Another area of biomedicine in which animals play an important role is research on the nervous system. The human brain contains 200 billion neurons, or nerve cells. These neurons connect with up to several hundred thousand other neurons, as well as with muscles and glands. Animals are being used to study neuron development and function. While tissue cultures, brain slices, or simple vertebrate neuronal systems can be used for such studies, researchers in this field say there is no adequate substitute for living animals. An understanding of the very complex functions of the human and animal brain in health and disease still depends on the use of animals in this specialized field of research.

Memory Research

It is estimated that 5 percent of people over the age of sixty-five have severe memory problems or loss of memory and cognition. Another 10 percent are believed to have mild to moderate cognitive or awareness problems. Moreover, certain conditions or diseases, such as Alzheimer's disease and Korsakoff's syndrome, affect mental function and can cause extreme memory loss as well as bizarre behavior.

Alzheimer's disease is mental deterioration accompanied by memory loss. Korsakoff's syndrome, a group of signs and symptoms that indicate psychosis, occurs in those with severe alcoholism. The symptoms are disorientation, falsification of memory (lying), and hallucinations.

Animal research has added much to our understanding of these two diseases since Alois Alzheimer, a German neurologist, announced his findings on the disease, and Sergei Sergeyevich Korsakoff, a Russian physician, stated his theories on the disease bearing his name. Both of these scientists conducted their research in the late nineteenth century.

Most of the data on neurotransmitters involved in these two diseases have been obtained from studies on the brains and nervous systems of chimpanzees. These nonhuman primates are closer to human beings than other animals, which explains their value in neurological and other biomedical research. Chimpanzees have age-related losses in memory just as human beings do. An important finding in this field of research was that memory impairment with advancing age first appears as failure of *immediate* memory. That is, a person may not remember the day's date but may be able to recall an event that happened years ago.

Clonidine, a chemical used as a neurotransmitter (a substance that transmits nerve impulses), has improved the memories of macaques, short-tailed monkeys native to northern Africa, Japan, and southeastern Asia. The drug has also been effective in improving the memories of patients suffering from Korsakoff's syndrome. Researchers believe that memory studies on animals may offer an approach to the eventual treatment of Alzheimer's disease.

While tissue cultures, biochemical methods, and brain imaging in human beings provide some alternatives to the use of experiments with animals, animals are still necessary for this type of biomedical research. The promising field of neural transplantation for the treatment of Alzheimer's disease and Parkinson's disease requires the use of animals. Since this area of biomedical research also requires the use of a large number of animals, neuroscientists are especially targeted by antivivisectionists and animal rights advocates.

One of the issues in the use of animals in research is the pain caused by experiments. There is no question that many experiments cause pain to laboratory animals. In fact, the very purpose of some experiments is to induce pain to learn more about this phenomenon common to both animals and human beings.

Pain is a common symptom of disease and injury. Medical and veterinary researchers seek ways to reduce or minimize the pain and discomfort suffered by laboratory animals. Researchers have developed techniques that are as humane as possible within the context and goal of an experiment. For instance, they have learned that the slightest reflex movement of a rat's tail indicates discomfort or pain when something is done to the animal. Reflex behavior, such as the tail flick, is a useful tool in judging how effective a certain analgesic, or painkiller, is in managing pain.

Many experiments involving pain can be performed on anesthetized animals. However, these experiments are performed when anesthetics will not interfere with the objectives of the particular experiment.

Animals have benefitted from some pain experiments performed on human beings. For example, certain psychophysical studies conducted on human beings have been repeated in animals. These experiments have made it possible for neurology researchers to trace nerve fibers from the skin, muscles, and internal organs. Each of these nerve fibers is a specific carrier of pain signals. These studies enabled researchers to explore the passage and transformation of pain signals in anesthetized animals.

PSYCHIATRIC AND PSYCHOLOGICAL STUDIES
Monkeys, chimpanzees, and other nonhuman primates are important subjects for certain medical and behavioral studies, but their use has been condemned as cruel and inhumane. Especially censored are experiments in which the nonhuman primates are subjected to electric shocks and other trauma. This type of experiment is known as a "learned helplessness study." The state of helplessness

in which this kind of experiment places a monkey or ape is, according to researchers, similar to the state of depression in which a human being feels helpless and hopeless.

Not so, say many opponents of these experiments. They do not accept the relationship between human depression and the collapse state in the monkeys or apes caused by electric shock or some other trauma. Besides, the animals undergoing such painful experiments do not show any symptoms associated with human depression. They do not suffer a loss of sleep, they do not have appetite problems, they do not have the suicidal tendencies associated with severe depression. Thus, according to animal rights activists, these experiments contribute little to an understanding of the complexities of human anxiety and depression. All these experiments achieve, according to opponents, is to produce reactions in terrified or tortured animals, symptoms reminiscent of what used to be called shell shock in combat soldiers.

Animals have been used in both biomedical and behavioral studies in American and Russian space programs. Monkeys, chimpanzees, dogs, rats, and mice preceded human astronauts into outer space. The first animal into outer space was Laika, a Russian dog, that orbited the earth in 1957. But she did not return to earth, for the space capsule in which she rode, *Sputnik II*, disintegrated five months later.

In 1960, two more Russian dogs, Belka and Strelka, were rocketed 200 miles above the earth in a space capsule. Russian scientists obtained important information from the animals in these early space flights. They learned much about the effects of acceleration, deceleration, weightlessness, and exposure to cosmic rays. An important question was whether exposure to cosmic rays would affect the breeding ability of an animal or human being. Another important question was whether such exposure would cause genetic mutations. Strelka's exposure to cosmic rays did not affect her reproductive ability. Five months after her memorable flight into outer space, she gave birth to a litter of normal puppies. Pushinska, one of the pups, was given to President John F. Kennedy as a pet for his daughter.

Seven chimpanzees were chosen to be the first non-human primates to be sent into space in the American space program. They were known as the "Astrochimps." Chimpanzees were selected for this project for several reasons: (1) they were intelligent and cooperative animals; (2) they were nearly human in size; and (3) they had a reflex action time close to that of humans, seven-tenths of a second for the chimps and five-tenths of a second for the average man.

The first chimp into space was Ham. He rocketed 155 miles above the Caribbean Sea on February 1, 1961. His capsule traveled on an arc to a point 420 miles from the launching pad. When Ham's capsule was recovered from the sea near the Bahama islands, he was found to be in good condition, none the worse for his exciting flight through outer space. Ham, a chimpanzee, age three years, eight months, born in the Cameroons in Africa, was the first primate to soar into outer space.

ACQUIRED IMMUNE DEFICIENCY SYNDROME (AIDS)

Chimpanzees have also been used in research on acquired immune deficiency syndrome, or AIDS. (A syndrome is a group of signs and symptoms that characterize a disease.) A disease somewhat like AIDS is simian acquired immune deficiency syndrome (SAIDS) seen in rhesus monkeys. It led researchers to believe that these monkeys could be used for AIDS research. The SAIDS virus was isolated, infection studies were done, and efforts to develop a vaccine began and are making progress.

But AIDS research is a different story. While chimpanzees have been infected with the human immunodeficiency virus (HIV), the virus that causes AIDS, they have not developed full-fledged AIDS. Instead, they develop flulike symptoms rather than the complications seen in AIDS. Researchers have other problems in using chimpanzees as models. First, these primates are becoming scarce; they are classified as an endangered species. AIDS-infected chimpanzees must be kept in isolation, which presents difficulties. These primates are very social animals and isolation is an extremely stressful experience for them. Furthermore, provisions of the Animal Welfare Act specify that nonhuman primates must be kept in an environment that will not cause them any physical or psychological harm.

Researchers say that the ability of HIV to undergo changes has interfered with the development of an AIDS vaccine. But progress has been made in developing a vaccine for the monkey immunodeficiency syndrome, SAIDS. About all that can be said for the AIDS animal research is that its methodology can be useful in human clinical trials. A presidential commission that studied the problem stated in its report, "The lack of appropriate animal models for HIV research makes the application of animal research to humans uncertain." The knowledge acquired about AIDS, its prevention and symptomatic treatment, comes from in vitro research (*in vitro* means outside the living body and in an artificial environment) and clinical trials with human patients. But animals are still being used in AIDS research.

A recently discovered virus, known as feline T-lymphotropic lentivirus, causes a disease in cats that has some similarity to AIDS. In its structure, the virus resembles HIV. However, there are some major differences, one being the fact that the virus cannot be analyzed genetically. Some researchers think that cats infected with this virus may provide useful models for research on certain aspects of AIDS.[1]

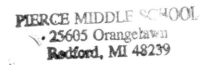

Cancer Research

Thousands of animals have been used in cancer research, with rodents playing an important role, but the value of animals in this field of research has been questioned. While human cancer is basically the same as that found in mice and rats, there are significant differences that warrant a different approach to research applicable to human beings.

Many cancer experiments involve the use of cell cultures, biochemical or other in vitro techniques, and computer models. Cancer research projects usually begin with in vitro studies that utilize either human or rodent cells. Later in the project, animal in vitro studies take over in the assessment of the causes of cancer, the biology of metastasis (the transfer of tumors from one organ or part of the body to another not directly connected to it), and the interaction of a tumor with the body's defense mechanisms.

Chemotherapy is a major treatment of cancer based on results of animal tests. A recent technique involves the use of human tumors kept in cell culture to screen drugs for safety and effectiveness. But the program for the frequency of use and the way to administer the drugs, such as orally or intravenously, are tested on animals. Animal studies are vital for determining the toxicity of a cancer drug. The evaluation of "methods for safely administering drugs directly into the central nervous system to treat certain brain tumors" is another important example of the use of animals in this field of biomedical research. Primates are used as animal models in the later stages of these experiments.[2]

Another important use of animals in cancer research is in the work done on chemotherapy for treating childhood leukemia. Untreated leukemia is usually fatal. Animals have been used in the development and testing of chemotherapeutic agents used in treating this disease.

Almost every facet of present cancer management

40

methods, as well as the advances made in this field, has somewhere along the line involved the use of animals. The data obtained from animal research are important for their application to cancer diagnostic tests and the treatment of both human beings and animals. But animal rights advocates, and some scientists, call for either restrictions on the use of animals in cancer research or their total elimination. Most cancer researchers say such measures would seriously disrupt or close down valuable cancer research. They argue that no currently available alternative can completely replace testing on animals in this important research field.

Animal research has produced benefits for various animals. Vaccines for canine distemper, feline panleukopenia (cat distemper), parvovirus, infectious canine hepatitis, leptospirosis (a bacterial disease that affects dogs and other animals and occurs in two forms: canicola fever and Weil's disease), tetanus, equine encephalitis, Bang's disease (brucellosis in human beings), and heartworm infestations have all been produced as a result of animal experiments. Millions of dogs, cats, and other animals have profited from these vaccines.

Especially important for both human beings and animals was the development of a vaccine against Bang's disease in dairy cattle and rabies in dogs. These two diseases are transmissible to human beings.

There are three types of brucella organisms: *Brucella abortus*, the cattle type; *B. melitensis*, affecting goats; and *B. suis*, found in swine. (Brucella organisms have also been found in deer, bison, and some other animals.) The brucella organisms were named after Dr. David Bruce, a British army surgeon who isolated *Brucella melitensis* in goat milk served to British soldiers on the island of Malta in 1887. (The disease in human beings is sometimes called Malta fever, or undulant fever.)

The development of a vaccine against this debilitating

disease was important for two reasons: (1) it prevented the loss of dairy calves and (2) it reduced the incidence of the transmission of this disease to farmers and others who drank raw milk.

Other research benefitting animals includes the development of vermicides for internal parasites, improvements in animal nutrition, invention or development of new surgical instruments and techniques (for example, use of staples in place of sutures for closing a surgical or other wound, which was demonstrated on dogs and other animals), and advances in the diagnosis and treatment of animal diseases.

In addition to the use of staples for closing wounds, an electrocautery hemostat has been invented for use on both animals and human beings. A hemostat is an instrument for constricting a blood vessel to check the flow or escape of blood during an operation. The hemostat is an old instrument, as is the electrocautery device, which has been in existence for about thirty-five years. Dr. Edward A. Lottick, a physician in Kingston, Pennsylvania, found a way to combine the two in his invention, the electrocautery hemostat.

Dr. Lottick's instrument was tried out on sheep obtained from the Animal Research Center in Hershey, Pennsylvania. The electrocautery hemostat proved to be quick and efficient. It enabled the surgeon to grasp and cauterize a bleeding vessel without changing hands or instruments, making the procedure much faster, and it was more efficient in diminishing blood loss. Both human beings and animals benefit from the use of this instrument.

It can be seen from this brief account that advances and achievements made in human and animal health have resulted from the use of animals in biomedical and behavioral research. More than eight hundred such advances and achievements depended on animal studies or experiments, according to an American Medical Association report.

The cast of animals used in research consists of numerous species and roles. Dogs, as noted earlier, were instrumental in the discovery and development of insulin. Procedures for the transplantation of organs involved dogs, primates, and other animals. A vaccine against acute hepatitis B was developed with the help of chimpanzees and other primates.

But these and other medical and veterinary advances are thrust aside by animal rights advocates and antivivisectionists. Even more moderate organizations, such as the Medical Research Modernization Committee (MRMC), cast a critical eye on the continued use of animals in biomedical research. They advocate the substitution of alternatives. While the MRMC admits that in vitro techniques are no substitutes for use of whole animals, alternatives "can be powerful tools for studies at the cellular level, particularly when human tissues are used."[3]

The charges against the use of animals in research range from the infliction of pain and suffering to performance of unnecessary experiments to irrelevancy to human beings. Consequently, researchers have been forced to defend their work against a strong and well-financed animal rights movement.

The National Association for Biomedical Research reported that animal rights groups, such as the People for the Ethical Treatment of Animals (PETA) and the Animal Liberation Front (ALF), have severely hampered biomedical research through theft of animals, destruction of valuable research equipment and records, fire bombing, and threats of bodily harm and even death to researchers. (The philosophy, policies, and tactics of animal rights organizations are covered in a later chapter.)

Physicians say there is justification for the use of animals in biomedical research. In the paper, *Use of Animals in Biomedical Research: The Challenge and Response,* the American Medical Association stated that animal research is essential for the improvement of the health and welfare of the American people. The AMA opposes any legislation or social action that will limit or restrict such use of animals.[4]

According to the AMA, the use of animals in biomedical research is supported by most Americans. However, they want assurances that laboratory animals are treated humanely and are used only when necessary. The AMA believes that animal rights advocates have exploited this public concern and have used it to impede, degrade, or eliminate important biomedical research. Many distinguished scientists and physicians think that the tactics and rhetoric of PETA, ALF, and the antivivisection societies will seriously compromise the future of biomedical research if these organizations are allowed to continue with their harassment and obstructive actions.

The contributions to human health and welfare made by animal research have not been exaggerated or overstated, according to the AMA. These contributions have received world recognition. Fifty-four of the seventy-six Nobel Prizes in medicine and physiology since 1901 have been awarded to scientists for discoveries that involved the use of animals. These discoveries included breakthroughs in the diagnosis, treatment, and prevention of both human and animal diseases.

The National Association for Biomedical Research (NABR) has more than three hundred institutional members. Seventy percent are universities with medical or veterinary schools or substantial biomedical research programs. The NABR insists that its members are concerned about the proper treatment of animals used in research programs. It has charged the animal rights movement with resorting to "visceral images with spoken half-truths, lies, and emotional invectives." According to the NABR, animal rights advocates try to portray biomedical researchers as uncaring or unfeeling people who are motivated solely by research grants, the need to publish, and profits.

The use of animals in biomedical and behavioral research has opponents in both the animal rights movement and the scientific community. Some call for the total use of alternatives, while others say that the use of animals should be reduced or limited. The same is true in the next category of the animals in research controversy: the testing of consumer products on animals.

Consumer Product Testing

Animals are widely used to test the safety and efficiency of chemicals and other consumer products. Tests are conducted on products such as floor wax, detergents, pesticides, soaps, shoe polish, shampoos, and drugs.

CONSUMER PRODUCT TESTS

Acute toxicity tests are tests that usually consist of administering a single dose of the product or chemical in a concentration high enough to produce toxic responses or death. One such test is the LD/50 (lethal dose/50) test, in which one-half of the test animals can be expected to die.

Eye and skin irritation tests involve a single exposure to a substance or product. They are aimed at providing warnings to users of the product for the handling of the product or lists of harmful effects in case of misuse or accidental exposure. The most common procedure to test for irritation is the Draize test, one that has been targeted for elimination by PETA and other animal rights groups.

Repeated, or long-term chronic, toxicity tests consist

of exposing an animal to a product or substance for periods of two weeks to more than a year. These tests are aimed at determining the effects of long-term exposure to drugs or other products that may be used for months or years by a consumer. Rodents are used for these tests.

Carcinogenicity tests consist of exposing an animal to chemicals or substances for most of the animal's lifetime. The purpose is to detect any carcinogens in the substance or product. Mice and rats are used in these tests.

Reproductive toxicity tests involve a variety of procedures aimed at determining the presence of substances that might cause infertility, miscarriages, or birth defects. Rabbits and rats are used in these tests.

Neurotoxicity tests involve a variety of doses and exposures to a substance or product. The purpose is to determine any toxic effects on the nervous system, such as changes in behavior, lack of coordination, motor disorders, and learning disabilities in the test animals.

Mutagenicity tests are aimed at learning whether specific substances can cause any changes in the genetic material of cells. (In the case of the drug thalidomide, the drug did not cause any mutations or deformities in test animals; the reverse was true when the drug was given to pregnant women.)

Most of these tests require the use of large numbers of animals. There are different estimates as to the total used on a yearly basis. Since the use of mice and rats in biomedical research and testing is not regulated by the Federal Animal Welfare Act, the number used is not reported. Thus, the figures given by various organizations may be considered to be "guesstimates" rather than true estimates. They range from several million animals per year to as many as 10 million.

The cosmetic industry, in particular, has been attacked by animal rights organizations for its use of large numbers of animals, mostly rabbits, to test cosmetics.

These consumer products, as well as food and drugs, are regulated under the provisions of the federal Food, Drug and Cosmetic Act and its amendments. While the law does not specify what tests a manufacturer must conduct on its products, it does require proof of the safety of a product and its ingredients. The FDA, EPA, and Consumer Product Safety Commission may require animal testing of a consumer product.

Manufacturers have relied on animals to test the safety of their products for what they believe to be valid reasons. One is, of course, safety. Another is protection of the manufacturer from lawsuits. If no testing was performed, a manufacturer would be compelled by law to print this warning on the product label: WARNING: THE SAFETY OF THIS PRODUCT HAS NOT BEEN DETERMINED.

Obviously, no manufacturer wants to have such a label on its products. The product would self-destruct, for only a few people might buy it, mainly those who could not read the label or those who ignore labels.

In defending themselves against attacks by PETA and other animal rights groups, cosmetic manufacturers argue that the safety of consumers is a prime concern and the main reason for the use of live animals to test products. Consumers should believe they can use cosmetics without experiencing any harmful effects, say the manufacturers. Also, employees handling cosmetic materials should be able to do so with safety. Some manufacturers maintain that animal testing is the most effective way to ensure the safety of a product and to comply with FDA regulations. While some alternatives are available, they are not yet reliable enough to eliminate the use of animals completely.

On the other hand, PETA and other animal rights groups say the use of animals for testing consumer products is not only cruel but unnecessary. They point to new technologies that have provided alternatives to animal testing, techniques that not only are humane but are cheaper and more exact. They cite in vitro studies, computer assays, simulated tissue and body fluid level measurements, mass spectrometry, and gas chromatography as alternatives. (PETA was responsible for ending the use of the Draize test by some major cosmetic and consumer products manufacturers.)

THE DRAIZE TEST

The Draize test, which tests for eye and skin irritation, was named after Dr. John Draize, an English researcher and senior author of a paper describing the test. This controversial test was originally developed for use in England but soon became a standard test in the United States, Canada, and other countries. It was sanctioned but not ordered by the FDA as a test that would meet a requirement of the Food, Drug and Cosmetic Act, which states that cosmetics "be free of deleterious or poisonous substances."

Rabbits are used in the Draize test because their eyes are especially sensitive. Also, they have no tear ducts; they cannot wash test materials out of their eyes. In performing the test, a rabbit's head is placed in a stock to prevent the animal from scratching or pawing at the eye in which a substance has been placed. The lower lid of one eye is pulled down and away from the eye. Then the test substance, such as nail polish remover, shampoo, or mascara, is dropped into or smeared on the eye. The other eye acts as a control. Testers look for redness in the affected eye, edema (swelling), hemorrhage, and other signs of irritation. Corneal ulcers and blindness are often the result of the Draize test, depending on the materials used. The rabbits may be killed after a test or may be used in some other test.

In 1989, because of pressure by PETA, two major cosmetic manufacturers, Revlon and Avon, agreed to stop all testing of their products on animals. PETA's tactics consisted of organizing boycotts, promoting shareholder resolutions, and alerting the general public to the use and cruelty of the Draize test.

Other consumer product manufacturers were attacked by PETA and other animal rights groups. They included Procter and Gamble, American Home Products, Bristol-Myers-Squibb, and Colgate-Palmolive corporations. Procter and Gamble manufactures soaps and other household products. American Home Products makes Pam cooking spray, Black Flag pesticide, Sani-flush, and other products. Bristol-Myers-Squibb manufactures pharmaceuticals and over-the-counter drugs and medicines. Colgate-Palmolive makes toothpaste, soaps, detergents, and other products. All of these corporations relied on animals to test the safety of their products.

While some manufacturers have halted the use of animals for testing their products—or have at least reduced the number of animals used—others say they have no alternative but to continue animal testing. If they cannot prove the safety of their products, the FDA will resort to regulatory actions. Such action would also take place if there were a complaint about a product. The FDA has the authority to inspect manufacturing plants and the power to seize adulterated or mislabeled products. The Food, Drug and Cosmetic Act defines an adulterated product as one that "contains a substance which may make it harmful to consumers under customary conditions of use."

Opponents of the Draize test have charged that it not only is cruel and inhumane but is outdated and unreliable. But the acting director of the FDA's Center for Veterinary Medicine disagreed with this charge at a congressional hearing in 1986. The congressional committee was inquiring into the use of animals for product testing. The acting director testified that the Draize test was still the most reliable method of determining the potential "harmfulness or safety of a product instilled in the eye, such as ophthalmic drugs, devices or cosmetic products." He stated that alternatives could not replace the Draize test.[1]

Later, Dr. Frank Young, at that time the FDA commissioner, stated that "the responses and results of tissue or cell culture tests alone cannot, at the present time, be the basis for determining the safety of a substance." He added that certain tests should never be carried out on human beings. Therefore, and since at the present time no adequate alternatives exist, whole animal testing remains unavoidable.

FDA TESTING GUIDELINES

The FDA, like some other federal agencies, has issued guidelines for the use of animals in product testing. The agency believes that the proper use of in vitro tests can reduce the number of animals used for the development of a product. Manufacturers should thus develop and use in vitro tests. However, there may never be a total replacement for the Draize test because of the limitations of in vitro tests.

The agency believes that a quick and inexpensive test, despite its inability to detect everything, can be used early on in the developmental phase of a product. Such use can eliminate chemicals that fail to pass in vitro tests. This early detection could reduce the number of chemicals needed to be tested on animals.

In vitro techniques, based partially on prior animal tests, could also be used as the final safety test for a product. However, in vitro tests would be limited so that only a minor change in an active product ingredient needed to be made. But previous experience would be needed for a tester to draw the conclusion that a specific in vitro test was capable of detecting any likely changes caused by reformulations. Since the FDA has no testing requirements for the premarketing of cosmetics, the agency has not developed plans for that purpose.

52

In issuing these statements, the FDA pointed out that they were not to be regarded as regulations, but as scientific opinions.

THE CONSUMER PRODUCT SAFETY COMMISSION (CPSC)

The federal Consumer Product Safety Commission has jurisdiction over all nonmedical household products. It is the only federal agency that has any regulations dealing with tests for irritation caused by a product. In May 1980, the CPSC placed an embargo on the use of the Draize test, pending the results of a study on the use of anesthetics for the animals used in this test. The study revealed that a double dose of tetracaine administered to rabbits reduced the pain produced by the test material. The anesthetic did not affect the irritancy scores or results.

The CPSC has issued guidelines for the use of animals for product testing:

- No testing for eye irritancy if the substance is a known primary skin irritant.
- An ophthalmic anesthetic, such as tetracaine, should be used *before* placing any substance in a rabbit's eye.
- It is recommended that a tier-testing approach to reduce the number of animals be used. The gradual increase in the dose for animals until irritation is determined, instead of initial use of a larger number of animals for tests, is the goal of this approach. Also, rabbits used in skin irritation tests should not be placed in stocks. They should have access to water and food while a substance is on their skin.

The CPSC issued a statement in March 1988: "We believe that an adequate non-animal replacement exists either for the Draize eye irritancy test or other acute toxicity tests." The agency added that "non-animal tests presently under development are not yet at a stage where they can be validated prior to their incorporation into regulatory protocols.''

In general, the CPSC position on the use of animals in product testing is that manufacturers are not required to conduct animal tests. All they have to do is label their products in such a way that a consumer is alerted to any hazards posed by the product. While animal testing may be necessary in some cases, such testing should be limited to the *lowest feasible number of animals*. All precautions should be taken to eliminate or reduce pain and discomfort in the animals.

Animal rights advocates were quick to point out a discrepancy in the CPSC position. The agency stated that it does not require testing for nonmedical consumer products. It further stated that nonanimal alternatives were not yet an acceptable measure of consumer safety. Then what is? asked the animal rights advocates. Further confusing the public and manufacturers, the CPSC more or less admitted that the only safety standard it will accept is that demonstrated by animal testing.

More suggestions and recommendations regarding the troublesome Draize test have been put forth. The Interagency Regulatory Liaison Group issued the following:

- Substances known to be corrosive may be assumed to be eye irritants and therefore should not be used in the manufacture of consumer eye products.
- Only three rabbits should be used in the Draize test instead of the usual six to ten animals. However, if the test results are equivocal, more rabbits may be used.
- Anesthetics should not be used in most tests. But if the substance is likely to cause intense pain, local anesthetics may be used prior to the application of the substance.

None of the limitations, recommendations, or guidelines for the Draize test is acceptable to PETA and other animal rights groups. They want total elimination of the Draize test and the use of animals for any test. For them, there is no compromise on this issue.

Manufacturers continue to defend their use of the Draize test. They are still fearful of lawsuits in the absence of animal tests. This defensive position began in 1974, when a woman accidentally spilled some shampoo in her eyes while bathing. The shampoo caused burning and pain and the destruction of her corneal epithelium.

The FDA brought suit against the manufacturer on behalf of the victim. But the court ruled in favor of the manufacturer because the FDA failed to show that the shampoo was any more dangerous than others on the market. Also, under normal use, that is, in a diluted form, the shampoo would not have caused the damage it did in concentrated form. Since the woman dropped the container of shampoo, the use was not "normal." The court also ruled that test results obtained from rabbits could be extrapolated to human beings.

The pressures and tactics used by PETA have been successful in forcing some large product manufacturers to stop using the Draize test. Revlon, Avon, Fabergé, Mary Kay Cosmetics, and Amway Corporation all declared a moratorium on the use of animals for product safety testing. These corporations realized that if they did not stop using animals in their product testing, the animal rights activists would increase their pressures and engage in more demonstrations, boycotts, and possible violent actions.

In a letter to the author, the manager of Avon's Consumer Information Center stated that the corporation has ended all animal testing. The new testing program uses nonanimal laboratory tests, clinical tests on human beings, and a large data base of ingredients and products that had been previously tested. (It is assumed that the data base was assembled with findings from animal tests.) The letter writer pointed out that Avon was the "first major cosmetic company in the world to eliminate product testing on animals.''

In another letter to the author, the senior product information specialist at Amway Corporation stated, "Future product safety evaluations will proceed through a multi-tiered process." This process involves the analysis of raw material safety from suppliers and the scientific literature. The letter went on to state that "as they are evaluated and validated for Amway's line of products, non-animal in vitro techniques will be incorporated into our overall safety review program."

Not all of the major corporations that have curtailed or ceased animal testing have widely advertised that fact. Liability is still a major fear. There could be backlash from consumers because cosmetics or other products were not tested on animals. The point has been brought up that consumers suffering from a reaction or injury from the use of a product would have a relatively easy time proving negligence in court because of the absence of animal tests.

Small companies are especially vulnerable to censorship for testing their products on animals because their products are often nonessential items. Some small companies have stopped using animal tests; others have not. Yet it is alleged that the products of some of these small manufacturers contain more dangerous substances than those found in cosmetics and other products made by large corporations.

What about the corporations that supply the cosmetic and other manufacturers with raw materials? Do they test their materials? If so, how? Many of them do test their raw materials and on animals.

Some manufacturers have lashed back at the animal rights activists. They say they are dealing with irrational opponents. A spokesman for the Cosmetic, Toiletry and Fragrance Association, a trade organization, charged that the industry was forced to deal with "zealots who cannot comprehend that a child's life is more important than a dog's—who see nothing wrong with making a child the ultimate guinea pig."

In a way, the manufacturers are faced with a dilemma: Appease the animal rights activists and prevent boycotts and loss of sales or continue animal testing and avoid liability, but face more harassment from the animal rights movement.

Some industry leaders believe that Avon and the other corporations that gave up animal testing acted too hastily in capitulating to PETA and the other animal rights groups. Others think it wrong to allow well-organized and well-funded groups to use scare tactics and, in some cases, such as the actions of the Animal Liberation Front, terrorism to force business people to forego their responsibilities to the public and their respective industries.

The animal rights movement continues its crusade for the elimination of the Draize and other product tests. They campaign for state laws that will end or at least limit the use of animals for product testing. Some states are considering such laws. Maryland was the first to consider a law of this type. However, it was defeated in 1988 after heavy lobbying by the cosmetic industry. A pending Pennsylvania bill has a section entitled "Prohibited Tests." Under the provisions of this law, "A person may not subject a live animal to an eye irritancy test, including the Draize test, or to use a live animal in an acute toxicity test, including the LD/50 test, for the purpose of testing cosmetics or household products." Other states considering similar legislation are California, Connecticut, Illinois, and Massachusetts.

LD/50 TEST
Another animal test that has been condemned by the animal rights advocates is the LD/50 test. It provides an estimate of the amount of a toxic substance that causes the death of 50 percent of a group of laboratory animals. It

has been criticized as cumbersome, unreliable, and cruel. This test was developed in England in 1927 by a mathematician. Its original application was to estimate the toxicity level of very potent drugs, such as digitalis, diphtheria toxin, and insulin. Its opponents say it has outlived its use.

As many as 200 animals may be used in a single LD/50 test, most commonly for the oral testing of a substance or product. Rats or other laboratory animals are force-fed the substance via a stomach tube. Then the animals are observed for two weeks or until death. Animals that survive the test are usually killed later.

Other procedures utilizing the LD/50 test include the inhalation of a chemical or substance. Animals are forced to breathe the vapor or powder of a chemical or substance. Chemicals may also be applied to the skin of an animal in the test. Finally, there is a procedure in which a chemical or substance is injected into an animal's body. In all the tests, observers look for signs of poisoning: for example, bleeding from the eyes, nose, or mouth; difficulty in breathing; tremors; convulsions; paralysis; and coma.

Critics of the test say that it concentrates on *when* an animal dies and not so much on *why*. They maintain that knowing the lethal dose and nature of a chemical or substance that can be obtained from human studies is of greater value than the LD/50 test results, especially when treating poison victims. According to opponents of this test, it does not predict a lethal dose in human beings very accurately because of the difference between the human and animal species. Critics also say that the general idea of applying the toxic effects of a substance or product from animal tests to human beings is open to question. According to an FDA survey, use of the LD/50 test has declined by 96 percent since the 1970s.

More animals are used in the long-term, or chronic, toxicity tests than in the acute toxicity tests. Chronic tests may take up to five years and require the use of hundreds of animals. The decision to use the long-term test depends on the substance. Long-term tests are mainly used to test the toxicity of pharmaceuticals and chemicals on an extended exposure basis. Animals used in all forms of the LD/50 test are dogs, rats, hamsters, and guinea pigs.

TESTING SUBSTANCES FOR CARCINOGENICITY

There is disagreement as to the value of using animals to test chemicals and other substances for carcinogenicity, or the ability to produce tumors. Some scientists believe that cancer tests on animals actually provoke or induce unnaturally high levels of cell division. Such cell division is known to increase the risk of mutations leading to cancer. Some believe that the idea that there is no safe dose of a carcinogen should be reexamined. Many chemicals that cause cell division, and ultimately cancer, may be safe at lower dosages.

But these beliefs or opinions are challenged. The points raised are important, but some scientists say it is too early to change testing methods. More studies are needed. Also, when something works, let it alone. They allude to the fact that the present product testing system has adequately protected the public.

The debate about the value of testing chemicals and other substances on animals for carcinogenicity goes on. Some health authorities maintain that even if there is a difference between human and animal mechanisms or tissues, the fact remains that if a chemical causes cancer in an animal, there is a good chance it will do so in human beings. Animals have to be used for acute and chronic toxicity studies because it is unethical to expose human beings to potential carcinogens for twenty or thirty years. A case in point was the long-range exposure of workers to asbestos, a carcinogen.

The Humane Society of the United States, in condemning the use of the LD/50 test, stated that its results are of little value in diagnosis and treatment. This society argues that animal tests do not yield enough data on the following:

The poisonous dose of a chemical or substance
The prediction of poisoning signs and symptoms
The prevention or correction of overdose
The lethal or nonlethal dose of a chemical or substance
The poisoning risks to newborn babies and infants
The long-term, or cumulative, effect of a chemical or substance on the human body
The specific cause of death in laboratory animals
The specific organs affected by the chemical or substance [2]

The use of animals to test the safety of consumer products is one of the prime targets of animal rights advocates. They say the Draize and LD/50 tests must be stopped. They argue that alternatives are now available. But proponents of animal testing disagree. True, there are some in vitro techniques that are promising but not at the stage to totally replace animals. Therefore, the end of the use of animals in consumer product testing is not yet in sight. Much depends on the speed at which scientists discover, develop, and validate alternative methods to the Draize and LD/50 tests.

Considerable progress has been made in developing alternatives for animal testing and reducing the number and kinds of animals used in biomedical and behavioral research. But there is another field in which animals are used for experimentation that has attracted the attention of animal rights activists and antivivisectionists. It is the use of animals in schools, colleges, and universities. Especially under attack is the dissecting of animals in biology classes.

4

ANIMAL EXPERIMENTATION IN EDUCATION

Animal studies and experiments have been a part of biology courses for many years. The dissection of frogs, cats, and other animals has been a popular or unpopular learning tool, depending on the student, in high schools, colleges, and universities. Some students dissect an assigned animal, whether a frog, cat, or fetal pig, with interest and perhaps curiosity. Others do so reluctantly, even with strong feelings of revulsion or disgust. Still others refuse to dissect any animal.

The Federal Animal Welfare Act, discussed in the next chapter, requires that colleges and universities conducting animal studies or experiments register with the Department of Agriculture. But elementary and high schools are exempt from such registration. They are not monitored or inspected by any agents of the Department of Agriculture, the agency responsible for the enforcement of the Animal Welfare Act. This lack of monitoring has been the focus of animal welfare group campaigns against the use of animals in classrooms for a number of years.

While there is no federal control of the use of animals

in the classroom, the dissection of animals by students is condemned by humanitarians and antivivisectionists. Some years ago, the Animal Welfare Institute, Humane Society of the United States, and Canadian Council on Animal Care collaborated in drawing up the following guidelines for the use of animals in elementary and high schools:

- In biological procedures involving live organisms, species such as plants, bacteria, fungi, protozoa, worms, snails, or insects should be used whenever possible. Their wide variety and availability in large numbers, the simplicity of their maintenance, and relatively humane ways of disposing of them make them especially suitable for student work.
- No procedure shall be performed on any warm-blooded animal that might cause it pain, suffering or discomfort or otherwise interfere with its normal health. Warm-blooded animals include, besides man, all mammals and birds.
- No surgery shall be performed on any living vertebrate animal: i.e., mammal, bird, amphibian, reptile, and fish.
- No lesson or experiment shall be performed on a vertebrate animal that employs microorganisms that can cause disease in animals or human beings. No ionizing radiation, cancer-producing agents, toxic chemicals, drugs producing pain or deformity, extremes in temperatures, electric or other shock, excessive noise, noxious fumes, exercise to the point of exhaustion, overcrowding or other distressing stimuli shall be used on any animal.
- The study or observation of classroom animals must be directly supervised by a competent biology teacher who shall approve a project plan before a student begins work. The supervisor shall oversee all experimental procedures, be responsible for their non-hazardous nature (to animals and students), and shall

personally inspect experimental animals during the course of the project to ensure that their health and comfort are fully sustained.

- Vertebrate studies shall be conducted only in locations where proper supervision is available. This means either in a school or institution of research or higher learning. No vertebrate animal studies shall be conducted at home, other than observations of normal animal behavior, for example, how a pet dog or cat behaves.
- In vertebrate studies, palatable food shall be provided in sufficient quantity to maintain normal growth of the animal. Diets deficient in essential foods are prohibited. Food shall not be withdrawn from an animal for periods longer than twelve hours, and clean drinking water shall be available at all times and should not be replaced with alcohol or drugs.
- Bird eggs subjected to experimental manipulation shall not be allowed to hatch. The embryos shall be killed humanely no later than the nineteenth day of incubation. If normal egg embryos are to be hatched, then satisfactory arrangements must be made for the humane disposal of the chicks.
- In those rare instances where the killing of a vertebrate animal is deemed necessary, it shall be performed in an approved humane manner (rapidly and painlessly) by an adult experienced in such techniques.
- Projects involving vertebrate animals will normally be restricted to measuring and studying normal physiological functions, for example, normal growth, activity cycle, metabolism, blood circulation, learning processes, normal behavior, reproduction, communication or isolated organ techniques. None of these studies requires the infliction of pain.
- The comfort of the animal shall receive first consideration. All animals shall be housed in appropriate spacious, comfortable and sanitary quarters. Adequate provision shall be made for the care of the animals at all times, including weekends and vacation periods.

And all animals shall be handled gently and humanely
at all times.

These guidelines, while restricting the use of animals in
the classroom and calling for their humane treatment, do
not rule out animal experimentation. They and others
like them have been followed in American and Canadian
elementary and secondary schools. In the absence of
federal control and inspections, schools more or less police themselves. While animals still play an important role
in school biology courses, the trend is to study alternative
topics such as molecular biology and ecology.

Despite these and other guidelines for the use of
animals in elementary and high school classrooms and
biology laboratories, animal rights advocates and antivivisectionists want to eliminate the use of animals in education. The more moderate animal welfare organizations,
such as the Humane Society of the United States and the
Animal Welfare Institute, tolerate the use of animals for
instruction in schools, subject, of course, to guidelines that
emphasize the humane treatment of animals. But these
organizations, along with the more militant groups, want
to see the end of dissection in the classroom.

The dissection of animals in high schools attracted
national attention in 1987 when a California high school
student, Jenifer Graham, refused to dissect a frog. She
objected to the dissecting on moral grounds. Jenifer was
told that she would fail the biology course if she did not
dissect a frog. (She had an A grade in the course up to
this time.) She persisted in her refusal to dissect a frog
and her grade was lowered to D (later, it was raised to a
C). This low grade was unacceptable to Jenifer and her
parents. She brought suit against the local school board
for failing to offer an alternative to dissection.

The lawsuit dragged on for months at great cost to
the Grahams. Finally, a federal judge issued a ruling on
August 1, 1988. His ruling: dismissal of the charge against

the school board and a compromise for Jenifer. Since a frog's anatomy and physiology were part of the biology course, her knowledge of these systems could and had to be tested. But, according to the judge, since Jenifer did not like the idea of killing frogs for dissection, she need not dissect a frog provided by the school. She could dissect a frog that had died of natural causes, rather than a healthy one that had been killed for the purpose of dissection.

The judge's compromise for Jenifer was not much help. It meant that someone would have to go hunt for a frog that had died of natural causes. Few people have ever found such a frog. Most frogs die from predation or pollution or some other unnatural cause. The judge failed to realize that finding a frog dead from natural causes would be no easy task. In fact, it would be a matter of pure luck.

In the end, Jenifer's right to refuse to dissect a frog was upheld. So was the school's right to test a student's knowledge of a frog's anatomy and physiology on a real frog. An important result of the case was the enactment of a state law—the first of its kind—that upholds the right of a student under eighteen years of age to conscientiously object to dissecting an animal. This law specifically refers to educational projects "involving the harmful or destructive use of animals." Under the provisions of this law, a biology teacher and student may cooperate in developing an alternative to dissection.

Since Jenifer's case, more students have refused to dissect an animal, and there have been demonstrations against dissection. Students have been supported in their cause by parents and various animal rights organizations eager to see the end of dissection in schools.

In October 1991, PETA launched a full-scale, month-long antidissection campaign in schools across the country. PETA encouraged students to protest the dissection of animals in biology class units or laboratories. More than that, students were urged to let their school boards know that they did not want any "animal-based studies" in their classrooms.[1]

The revolt of students over the issue of dissection has caused school administrators and biology teachers to reevaluate this instructional tool. Some cogent questions are posed. While the dissecting of frogs in high schools dates to the early part of the twentieth century, is it really necessary today? Can't students learn just as much about animal anatomy and physiology from videotapes, take-apart models, and computer simulations?

It is true that there are some students who might profit from dissecting a frog or other animal. These are students who plan to become human or veterinary surgeons or pathologists, careers in which manual dexterity and dissecting techniques are of value. But opponents say it is not necessary for a student to acquire manual skills by dissecting; such skills, they say, can be obtained by performing surgery under the eye of an expert surgeon.

Millions of frogs are dissected every year in high school biology courses. Leopard frogs, *Rana pipiens pipiens*, are the species mainly used for dissection. They are a widely distributed species in North America, with a range that includes most of the United States (except the Pacific Coast) and areas extending deep into Canada and Mexico. This frog often lives some distance from water, mostly in meadows. It is in great demand, not only for dissecting but as fish bait. At one time, this frog played an important role in testing for human pregnancy, as did rabbits. The development of special pregnancy kits now precludes the use of frogs and rabbits for this purpose.

Undoubtedly the demand for leopard frogs for dissection has contributed to a decrease in their populations in some regions of the country. But there are other reasons for such losses—pollution, pesticides, drainage of swamplands, and prolonged droughts.

Frogs are not the only animals used for dissection,

although they are probably the most popular subjects. A bit down the popularity scale is the fetal pig; the cat is used more sparingly. Also dissected in schools are crayfish, grasshoppers, starfish, and other invertebrates.

The fetal pig is also used in college biology courses. Students use laboratory manuals to guide them in dissecting the pig. These exercises contain detailed descriptions and illustrations of the various systems of the fetal pig and step-by-step procedures for dissection. For instance, in the exercise on the urogenital system of the fetal pig, the biology student is given this advice: "Although you will dissect the reproductive system of only one sex, you should use another student's specimen to study the opposite sex."[2]

Many biology teachers and other educators believe that dissection is an important learning tool. They have what they consider to be valid reasons for including this controversial teaching technique in biology courses. One of their contentions is that dissecting gives a student firsthand knowledge of the internal structure of an animal. By dissecting a frog or fetal pig, for example, a student can see the relationship between various tissues; he or she can also feel the texture of animal tissue. Computer models and other alternatives cannot provide this experience. In dissection, a student learns about the relationship between the structure of an animal's body and its function. Finally, dissection allows a holistic approach to the study of animal anatomy and physiology.

But antivivisectionists and animal rights advocates are not impressed by these assertions. They feel that dissecting animals in schools must stop. Some opponents, such as PETA, say that animals should not be used for any purpose in the classroom. Others point out that dissecting an animal can be a very traumatic experience for a young student. Junior and senior high school students have been observed to run a gamut of emotions when faced with the assignment of dissecting a frog, pig, or other animal. They have shown fear, distaste, revulsion, and even horror. When these facts are taken into consideration, some opponents of dissection say it has no place in the modern school program. There is no valid reason to subject students to what, for many, is a disgusting or upsetting experience. Furthermore, according to opponents of dissection, modern technology has provided adequate substitutes for this outmoded and unwanted technique.

The pressure to abandon dissection and animal experimentation in colleges and universities, especially medical and veterinary schools, is gaining in strength. College students and animal rights groups protest the use of animals in education. A number of colleges and universities, as well as medical and veterinary schools, have reassessed their animal use programs.

A charge brought against college biology programs and medical and veterinary courses in which animal experiments are performed is that many of the experiments are "mindless duplications." They are unnecessary, they cause pain and suffering to animals, and they turn off students.

The American Antivivisection Society charges that a number of colleges and universities are guilty of violating provisions of the federal Animal Welfare Act. Such violations result in pain and discomfort to animals used in research or experimental programs in these institutions.

Included on the AAVS proscribed list are the University of Pennsylvania (this university's research laboratories were broken into by agents of the Animal Liberation Front and researchers threatened with bodily harm), University of California at Berkeley, Harvard University, Columbia University, Medical College of Wisconsin, University of Utah, University of Hawaii, Yale University, and University of Georgia.[3]

Many medical students are now using alternatives. The American Medical Student Association (AMSA) has taken the position that medical students who object to experimenting on animals be allowed to use alternatives. An AMSA argument is that students who object to human abortions would never be forced to undergo or perform such operations. Similarly, a student who is opposed to the use of animals for experimentation should not be forced to perform animal experiments. Today, some medical schools are allowing students to choose between animal experiments and suitable alternatives.

Some veterinary students also object to animal experiments. They are in a field in which animals may be not only subjects, but patients as well. Most veterinary schools operate hospitals or clinics. Nevertheless, they have been affected by the demands to limit or eliminate animal experiments as teaching tools in their physiology, pharmacology, and surgery courses. Veterinary educators are reassessing their curricula and teaching techniques as a result of pressures brought by students, antivivisectionists, and animal rights advocates. There are a number of alternatives now available for use by veterinary students. But can they totally replace animals in these specialized schools?

In most veterinary schools, according to a survey, students spend from four to seven hours a day in what has been described as "excessive mind-numbing lectures," physiology laboratories, and in practice surgery. Dr. Roy Pollock, director of the Center for Medical Information, New York State College of Veterinary Medicine, recommended a reduction in the amount of time that a student must spend in listening to lectures. According to Dr. Pollock, students need to use information, rather than merely commit it to memory.

More medical and veterinary educators now believe that substituting other procedures for the use of animals in research and experimentation will not dilute the quality and effectiveness of education. In fact, they point to some distinct advantages in the use of alternatives to traditional animal methods and techniques. The efficiency of alternative methods reduces the time required to set up an experiment, and those methods are easier to supervise. Most animal experiments take a lot of time and require more supervision.[4]

Can the use of animals as teaching tools be replaced by alternatives? As in the case of biomedical and behavioral research, this is a disputed point. Animal rights groups, antivivisectionists, and some educators say yes, and such alternative techniques are now available. Others say that alternatives cannot totally replace the use of animals in medical education, especially in veterinary medicine, because animals are the obvious models in this specialized field of education.

If animals are used for teaching purposes in the foreseeable future, they will not be unprotected. Animal studies and experiments in colleges and universities, as in other research facilities, are regulated by provisions of the Federal Animal Welfare Act. If colleges and universities violate these provisions, as charged by the American Antivivisection Society, then they are subject to penalties. Important provisions of this laboratory animal protection law, as well as other guidelines for the humane treatment and use of experimental animals, are presented in the next chapter.

ANIMAL PROTECTION
LAWS AND GUIDELINES

Prior to 1966, federal law did not protect laboratory animals. Most states had anticruelty laws, but they varied in the kind of protection offered, as well as in the penalties for violations. When the Federal Animal Welfare Act was passed by Congress in 1966, laboratory animals were given the protection humanitarians had been demanding for a long time. The use and treatment of laboratory animals were now regulated.

This important legislation was not whisked through Congress. There was considerable opposition to its form, phrasing, and provisions. Like Thomas Jefferson's Declaration of Independence, the Animal Welfare Act underwent many changes, deletions, and additions. It had a stormy passage through the Senate and House of Representatives. There were months of heated debate and compromise involving humanitarians, antivivisectionists, scientists, politicians, and government officials before the law was finally enacted, and it has since been amended several times.

ANIMAL WELFARE ACT (AWA) _____

This important federal animal protection law is administered and enforced by the United States Department of Agriculture's Animal and Plant Health Inspection Service (APHIS). In enacting this law, Congress pointed out that the use of animals was important to certain kinds of research intended to advance "knowledge of diseases, their treatment and cure, and injuries that can be sustained by both human beings and animals." Congress also noted that methods for testing substances were being developed that were expected to be faster, less expensive, and more accurate than some traditional animal tests. The reference in 1966 was to the development of alternatives still under investigation.

The AWA defines an animal as "any live or dead dog, cat, monkey (or other nonhuman primate), guinea pig, hamster, rabbit or such other warm-blooded animal, as the Secretary of Agriculture may determine is being used or is intended for use for research, testing or experimentation."

TYPES OF RESEARCH FACILITIES _____

A research facility is defined as any school (except elementary and high schools), institution, organization, laboratory, or person that uses or intends to use live animals for research or testing products. Also included in this definition is any person or organization or institution that receives funds under a grant, award, loan, or contract from a department or agency of the United States government for the purpose of research or product testing.[1] These research facilities fall into categories:

- *Federal and state facilities:* These include public institutions administered or funded by a state or federal agency.

- *Pharmaceutical manufacturers*: Research facilities of these manufacturers must be registered with APHIS, even if they are already registered under the federal Virus-Serum-Toxin Act.
- *Diagnostic laboratories or any facility performing laboratory functions*: These must register with the U.S. Department of Agriculture.
- *Educational research facilities above the secondary school level*: These must register and include colleges, universities, medical and veterinary schools, and biology classes conducting animal research or experimentation.
- *Marine mammal research facilities*: Facilities using seals, whales, or other marine mammals for behavioral, biomedical, or related studies must register with the USDA. Furthermore, if the marine mammal facility also exhibits marine mammals, it must obtain an exhibitor's license. The same standards of animal care and treatment apply to an exhibitor as to a research facility.
- *Federal research centers*: These do not have to register. However, they must comply with all the animal care and use standards of the Animal Welfare Act.
- *All schools below the college level*: These are exempt from registering with the USDA. However, the USDA discourages animal research or experimentation in elementary and secondary schools.
- *Small-scale diagnostic laboratories conducting studies on nonregulated animals, such as mice and rats*: These may apply for exemption from registering with the USDA.
- *Agricultural research stations conducting studies or tests or agricultural practices involving horses, cattle, sheep, or other livestock*: These are not required to register.
- *Research facilities using biologic specimens alone*: Facilities using dead animals or parts or organs thereof need not register with the USDA.
- *Institutions using nonregulated animals such as birds, domestic mice, and rats*: These are exempt, but they

must register if they use wild rodents, such as the field mouse or wood rat.

Registered research facilities are required to maintain accurate records on animal use. They must keep track of the purchase, sale, and identification of previous ownership of dogs and cats. (Monkeys, guinea pigs, hamsters, and rabbits are not included in this requirement.) No animal researcher or facility may purchase any dog or cat from anyone other than a licensed laboratory animal dealer. This important provision protects dog and cat owners from the unlawful use of their pets in a laboratory should a pet be stolen, lost, or turned over to a research facility by a publicly funded pound or animal shelter. According to PETA, each year 200,000 cats and dogs end up in laboratories under "pound seizure" laws.

THE CARE AND TREATMENT OF LABORATORY ANIMALS _____

Animal Welfare Act provisions are very specific about the care, treatment, and use of experimental animals. Under provisions of the law, the secretary of agriculture is authorized to formulate and put into effect standards for the humane care of laboratory animals. Among the standards now in force are minimum requirements for handling, housing, feeding, watering, sanitation, and protection from extremes in weather and temperatures.

Adequate veterinary care must be provided to all experimental animals. Animals must be separated by species when necessary for their safety. A research facility using primates must provide a physical environment conducive to the well-being of monkeys, chimpanzees, and other nonhuman primates. The Harlow experiments discussed in Chapter One were severely criticized because of the isolation of baby monkeys.

All experiments must be performed with a minimum

of pain. Animals must be given anesthetics, tranquilizers, or euthanasia as determined by a veterinarian. The person in charge of an experiment is responsible for considering the use of alternatives when an experiment is likely to cause intense pain or distress.

In those experiments likely to cause severe pain and distress, a veterinarian must be consulted in the planning of the procedure. In the planning stages, attention should be paid to the appropriate use of anesthetics or other painkillers. If it is necessary to withhold pain relievers for the validity of an experiment, then such withholding shall continue only for the minimum time it takes for the experiment. That is, once a result has been obtained, the animal should not be denied pain or stress relievers.

The secretary of agriculture may issue rules or regulations regarding the design and performance of an experiment or study. This means that a halt can be called to any experiment or research project by a federal inspector for the purpose of determining whether the standards set forth by the AWA are being followed. Animal rights advocates claim that the standards are not always enforced or that inspections are too infrequent.

An important amendment to the AWA requires all research facilities to establish an institutional animal committee. This committee is to be appointed by the director or chief executive officer of the research facility. The committee must have at least three members, and members must have the knowledge and ability to assess the quality of the care and treatment of laboratory animals being used in the facility. They must also be able to evaluate scientific practices as determined by the needs of the particular research facility.

One member of the committee must be a veterinarian. At least one member may not be affiliated in any way with the research facility other than as a member of the animal care committee. No member of the committee can be a member of the immediate family of a person affiliated with the research facility. A quorum is necessary for all formal actions and deliberations of the committee, including inspections of laboratory animals, facilities, and experiments.

This animal care committee is required to inspect—at least twice a year—all animal study areas and animal facilities. It must inspect and evaluate all experiments involving pain and stress. The condition of the laboratory animals must be noted to ensure compliance with the standards mandated in the AWA. Exceptions to the inspection requirements may be made by the secretary of agriculture if animals are studied or observed in their natural environment or if the study area is difficult to assess.

The committee is required to file a report with APHIS, certifying that such inspections have been conducted. The report must be signed by a majority of the committee members conducting the inspections. The report must include any violations of the AWA standards, with special attention paid to any deficient conditions in the care and treatment of animals. And any committee minority or dissident views of a committee member must be included in the report.

The committee notifies the research facility of any deficiencies or violations of the AWA standards. If, after receiving such notification, and given an opportunity to correct any deficiencies or violations, a research facility fails to comply with the committee's recommendations, the committee notifies the Animal and Plant Health Inspection Service of the violations.

Federal research facilities, such as the Centers for Disease Control in Atlanta, Georgia, must also establish an animal care committee. However, a federal research facility committee reports any deficiencies or violations to the head of the research facility rather than to APHIS.

Each federal research facility must provide for the training of scientists, animal technicians, and other personnel involved in the care, treatment, or use of laboratory animals. The training must include what constitutes humane practices of animal care and experimentation, and what research or testing methods minimize or eliminate the use of animals or reduce pain and distress.

If a federally funded research facility fails to comply with the AWA standards and regulations, it is put on notice by the Department of Agriculture. The facility must then bring its practices and animal care into compliance with the AWA standards. If a federal research facility fails to correct deficiencies and violations, federal support will be suspended or revoked, depending on the circumstances and nature of the violations.

The Animal Welfare Act carries penalties for anyone who interferes with someone performing his or her duties under the provisions of the law. Anyone who assaults, resists, opposes, impedes, intimidates, or interferes with anyone performing his or her duties under the AWA provisions is liable to a fine of a maximum of $5,000 or imprisonment for not more than three years or both. Whoever kills any person performing duties under the provisions of the AWA will be prosecuted under United States Code 18, the code that deals with murder.

The Animal Welfare Act has been amended several times. The latest amendment, enacted in 1990, is concerned with the welfare of guinea pigs, hamsters, and rabbits. It covers the humane handling, care, treatment, and transportation of these small laboratory animals.

The 1990 amendment revises the space requirements for these animals in cargo areas of aircraft. It also regulates ventilation and temperature control in those compartments. When too many animals have been packed into cages or spaces while being transported to research facilities, they have suffered from cramping, heat, cold, or poor stowage. The lack of adequate ventilation and extremes in temperatures, in particular, cause the deaths of guinea pigs, hamsters, and rabbits on their way to research laboratories.

However, the transportation industry has objected to the ventilation and temperature control requirements specified in the AWA amendment. Transportation officials maintain that full compliance is not possible because aircraft used in the transportation of small animals do not have mechanical ventilation or cooling systems in their cargo holds. Despite the objections, no changes were made in the 1990 amendment.

POUND SEIZURE LAWS

A number of states have enacted pound seizure laws that require publicly funded animal shelters or municipal pounds to turn unwanted dogs and cats over to research laboratories. A pound is a building or enclosure where stray or lost animals are kept. The term comes from an English word, *impound*, which means to hold or contain. Animals in municipal pounds, if not claimed within a specified time, may be put to sleep or turned over to a research facility.

Pound seizure laws are very controversial and have been condemned by animal rights groups, antivivisectionists, and animal welfare organizations. Campaigns are under way in various states to repeal such laws. New York State has repealed its pound seizure law, known as the Hatch-Metcalf Act (named after two New York state legislators), which was enacted in the 1950s. This law required the American SPCA to turn unwanted dogs and cats over to laboratories. It was repealed in 1987 when the New York legislature enacted a law protecting shelter or pound animals. This new law prohibits any dog pound, animal shelter, SPCA facility, dog protective association, dog control officer, peace officer, or employee of these organizations from releasing any dog or cat to a research laboratory.

Massachusetts has also repealed a law that required

municipal pounds and publicly funded animal shelters to turn animals over to research facilities. The Massachusetts State legislature also ordered its Public Health Department to establish regulations for the licensing of research facilities using cats and dogs for experiments or educational purposes. This provision includes research facilities exempt from registration with the USDA.

The new Massachusetts animal protection law also authorizes the Massachusetts SPCA and the Animal Rescue League to conduct a minimum of four annual inspections of research facilities. This law, unwelcome to researchers, has far-reaching effects for the protection of all animals in the state of Massachusetts.

Canada's Animals for Research Act, passed in 1969, has caused as much consternation and anger in that country as have pound seizure laws in the United States. Under this Canadian law, municipalities can provide animals for research purposes, providing the animals are strays or are unclaimed. In the fall of 1990, Canadian animal rights groups met with the Canadian minister of agriculture to discuss changes in the law. What the animal rights advocates want is the elimination of the provisions requiring municipal pounds to turn unwanted animals over to laboratories.

But Canadian researchers oppose such elimination. Some researchers at the University of Toronto argue that important research would be jeopardized by a lack of animals if they were not provided by municipal pounds; animals sold by laboratory animal breeders or dealers are expensive. The University of Toronto researchers conduct important research on cardiovascular diseases and diabetes, as well as organ transplants, on animals obtained from pounds. A spokesperson for the university researchers stated that it "was easy to say go to an alternative. But certain types of research and training are impossible without the real thing."

Various medical, veterinary, scientific, and animal welfare organizations in the United States and Canada have established guidelines for the humane care and use of laboratory animals. One is the *Guide for the Care and Use of Laboratory Animals,* published by the United States National Institutes of Health (NIH). The NIH guide has been approved by the governing board of the National Research Council, whose members are drawn from the National Academy of Sciences, National Academy of Engineering, and Institute of Medicine.

The stated purpose of the NIH guide is to "assist institutions in caring for and using laboratory animals in ways judged to be professionally and humanely appropriate."[2] The guide acknowledges the fact that researchers have both a scientific and an ethical responsibility for the humane treatment of laboratory animals. Also, according to the guide, the intent of research should be to provide information or data that will advance knowledge of immediate or potential benefit to human beings and animals. Scientists should, however, continue to seek and develop valid alternatives to animals. This guide is a primary reference put to use in both public and private research facilities and institutions.

The NIH guide presents a range of recommendations for the humane care and treatment of laboratory animals. These include veterinary care, housing, bedding, food, water, sanitation, surgery, postsurgical care, social environment for primates, restraints, and euthanasia.

In the matter of restraint, the guide advises that animals should be introduced to the restraint equipment (stocks or squeeze cages) before the experiment to prevent undue stress. The period of restraint should be the minimum needed for the purpose of the experiment. Prolonged restraint must be approved by the facility animal committee. Researchers must be alert to any lesions or illnesses that may develop during restraint. If these or other conditions occur, the animal must be treated by a veterinarian. If necessary, the animal should be temporarily or permanently removed from the stock or squeeze cage or other restraint device.

An important recommendation is the one concerning restricted activity of experimental animals. There are no hard-and-fast rules. Animals confined to a cage or restraint device may be somewhat limited in their activity. The NIH guide admits that "there are no unequivocal data relating the quality or quantity of an animal's activity to its physical or psychological well-being." According to the guide, restricting an animal to a cage does not necessarily limit the amount of activity it has. A mouse can get enough exercise running around a cage or walking or running on an exercise wheel. Larger animals, though, do need to be exercised.

The NIH guide provides the responsible researcher with important recommendations for the care, treatment, and use of laboratory animals. The emphasis is on reducing the pain, distress, and discomfort of animals, while recognizing that these factors may be the focus of some experiments.

THE CANADIAN COUNCIL ON ANIMAL CARE (CCAC)

Most Canadians are as concerned as Americans about the welfare of laboratory animals. The Canadian Council on Animal Care was established in 1968. Its stated purpose is to improve the care and treatment of laboratory animals. The CCAC works in cooperation with both scientific and humanitarian organizations. It recognizes the changes that have taken place in the scientific community and among animal welfare advocates, especially the growth of the animal rights movement.

The CCAC approach to the issue of animal research

has merited the support of the Canadian scientific community, research granting agencies, government agencies, colleges, universities, and the Canadian Federation of Humane Societies. This organization also has the approval and cooperation of the Canadian Medical Research Council and the Natural Sciences and Engineering Research Council for its rational approach to the use and treatment of animals in research.

With assistance from the Canadian Federation of Humane Societies, the CCAC established standards for animal care and experimentation. These standards and recommendations are presented in a two-volume work: *Guide to the Care and Use of Experimental Animals.*[3] Canadian researchers, like their American counterparts, must conduct their research according to specified standards and regulations.

According to the CCAC, researchers must conform to the principles and guidelines set down in the *Guide.* The use of animals should only be considered after researchers have sought and failed to find suitable alternatives. Researchers need to use the best methods on the fewest possible animals. Proposed research projects or experiments should be justified in terms of the declared objectives. Furthermore, the design or plan of a research project or experiment must provide every practicable safeguard for the animals.

CCAC principles of animal research require that there be a reasonable expectation that the results will make significant contributions to human and animal health. Moreover, Canadian researchers have the moral obligation to abide by the humanitarian concept that experimental animals are not to be subjected to needless pain or suffering.

The CCAC principles, like those set forth in the American Animal Welfare Act, dictate that if pain and suffering are necessary aspects of an experiment or study, then they should be held to an absolute minimum, in both intensity and duration. Also, any animal observed to be in intense pain or distress that cannot be eased after an experiment should be humanely and immediately destroyed.

Experiments involving the withholding of food and water should be of short duration, and they should have no lasting effect on the health of an animal. Prolonged restraint should be used only after alternative methods have been considered and found impractical for the specific experiment. The method of restraint must provide an animal with the opportunity to assume normal positions such as standing, sitting, or lying down. An animal must not be forced to lie or stand or crouch in one position without relief or rest periods. In general, there must be a minimum of physical and mental discomfort.

The CCAC guidelines discourage painful experiments or multiple surgical procedures aimed solely at instructing students or demonstrating some established scientific fact or principle—in short, no repetitive or unnecessary experiments. Such experiments are unjustified, according to the CCAC, because there are alternatives, such as use of audiovisual aids and computer models.

Contrary to what the public is led to believe by the allegations of animal rights advocates and the emotional literature disseminated by antivivisectionists, researchers are required to adhere to the standards of the Animal Welfare Act or, in the case of Canadian researchers, recommendations and rules set forth by the Canadian Council on Animal Care.

Animal rights advocates and antivivisectionists are not satisfied with the protection offered by the Animal Welfare Act and the Canadian Council on Animal Care guidelines. According to opponents, the guidelines and standards do not go far enough—they allow for too much pain and distress. Furthermore, according to animal rights activists, the provisions of the Animal Welfare Act are not followed in every case, and inspections by agents are too infrequent. Opponents maintain that, all in all, the animal protection system is not all that researchers and government agencies would like the public to believe; it has flaws that cause pain and suffering to animals.

Accordingly, animal rights advocates want more stringent laws on the federal, state, and local levels. Efforts to obtain such laws are under way. In 1990, for example, animal rights activists in Cambridge, Massachusetts, demanded the enactment of a local ordinance that would further regulate animal research beyond that mandated in the Animal Welfare Act.

The proposed ordinance establishes an advisory committee that regulates all animal experiments within the Cambridge city limits. This law could affect more than 50,000 animals used at Harvard University, the Massachusetts Institute of Technology, and some local companies conducting research.

Animal rights advocates and antivivisectionists who favor this ordinance—and others like it—believe it makes up for deficiencies they claim exist in the Federal Animal Welfare Act, the NIH guidelines, and other animal care and use guidelines. As an example, domestic mice and rats, which constitute about 90 percent of the laboratory animals used in the Cambridge area, are not protected by the AWA or any other law.

The Massachusetts SPCA maintains that most of the monitoring and inspecting of animal research facilities by state and federal inspectors is inadequate. The inspections deal mainly with a research facility's physical plant and housing of animals, rather than with their pain and suffering.

There is opposition to the Cambridge ordinance and laws like it. First of all, opponents point out that the 1985 amendment to the Animal Welfare Act requires research facilities or institutions to establish "watchdog" committees to monitor experiments and the care and treatment of animals. The opponents argue that all registered research facilities do have such committees and are complying with the standards set down in the act. Therefore, laws like the Cambridge ordinance are unnecessary.

The pressures and actions of animal rights activists are of concern to politicians. The issue is double-edged. Stronger laboratory animal protection laws can have a direct effect on the availability of animals for important research. They can also affect psychological and pharmaceutical tests and studies. In such cases, the public would be the loser.

The animal rights movement is steadily growing in membership and influence, as well as funding. Many members of animal rights groups are articulate voters; politicians realize that the fight to influence the public's attitude toward the use of animals in research is a serious one. Politicians can no longer dismiss the animal rights advocates as do-gooders or fanatics. A wrong move by a politician regarding the animals in research issue can be fatal in an election.

Nevertheless, bills dealing with one phase or another of the issue have been introduced into state legislatures and Congress. Senator Howell Hefflin, a Democrat from Alabama, introduced into Congress the Animal Research Facility Protection Act of 1990. Hefflin's bill would amend the Animal Welfare Act, making it a federal crime for anyone stealing or causing the loss of any animal from a research laboratory. The bill would also outlaw the destruction of property and equipment, vandalism or theft, and entry into a laboratory with the intent to destroy equipment or research records.

Since the actions mentioned in the Hefflin bill would be federal crimes, the FBI could employ its vast resources against those persons or organizations breaking the law. The bill also provides that the secretary of agriculture and the United States attorney general could conduct a study of the "extent and effects of domestic and international terrorism on animal research, production and processing facilities."

Researchers endorse Hefflin's bill. After more than a decade of demonstrations, laboratory break-ins, vandalism, destruction of equipment and valuable records, and threats of bodily harm and even death, researchers feel that it is time they received some relief and protection.

Animal rights advocates welcome House of Representatives Bill 1389, introduced into the House by Robert Torricelli, Democrat from New Jersey, and endorsed by more than thirty members of Congress. Torricelli's bill is designed to "promote the dissemination of biomedical information through modern methods of science and technology, and to prevent the duplication of experiments on live animals, and for other purposes."

HR 1389 states that "overwhelming numbers of animals are used in duplicate research because of the research community's inability to determine what research has been performed."[4] This situation, according to the bill, has resulted from an inefficient system of storage and dissemination of medical information. The bill recommends the establishment of a National Center for Research Accountability. This center, along with a "comprehensive literature search before approval of federal funding," would spare millions of animals from pain and suffering caused by duplication of experiments.

Regardless of the Animal Welfare Act, NIH and other animal care and use guidelines, and various proposed state laboratory animal protection laws, animal rights activists and antivivisectionists continue to pressure and harass researchers. The major organizations that oppose the use of animals in biomedical research, product testing, and education are examined in the next chapter.

THE OPPOSITION TO ANIMAL EXPERIMENTATION IN RESEARCH

The appearance of animal rights and animal liberation groups in the 1970s precipitated a drastic change in the arguments and tactics in the crusade to eliminate cruelty to animals. These new animal welfare organizations took over the leadership of the movement, which began in the nineteenth century. The passive policies of the traditional humane societies were jettisoned, and a more militant and aggressive approach emerged.

It is generally agreed that the rapid rise and expansion of the modern animal rights movement received their impetus from the arguments of three books. These were *Animals, Man and Morals* by Godlovitch, Godlovitch, and Harris; *Victims of Science* by Richard Ryder; and *Animal Liberation* by Peter Singer. These books served as a call to action and attracted hundreds of recruits to the new animal rights movement.

Singer's book was the bible of many of the animal rights activists, providing them with philosophical arguments and guidelines for the liberation of animals. At the time, Peter Singer was professor of philosophy and bioethics at Monash University in Melbourne, Australia. *Bioethics* is the study of the ethical and moral questions involved in the application of new biological and medical findings, for example, genetic engineering and drug research.

People's misuse of animals, according to Singer, causes pain and suffering comparable to that inflicted on blacks by antebellum Southerners. In his book, *Animal Liberation*, he charges that human beings are "specieists." He claims that the mistreatment of animals is condoned by human beings because it promotes the "trivial interests of their own species." He maintains that the cruelties inflicted on animals in research continue because of the general acceptance of this "specieism." Because of this acceptance, cruelties to animals are practiced that would not be tolerated if inflicted on human beings.[1]

Singer also questions other uses of animals, such as for food and fiber. His book was important to the developing animal rights movement for two reasons. First, he presented the cause of animal exploitation on a more intellectual plane than did the older, more traditional, animal welfare groups. He zeroed in on the ethical and moral aspects of the exploitation and mistreatment of animals. And second, his book attracted the attention of activists seeking a new cause. These are people who bring to the animal rights movement the same dedication, commitment, and aggressiveness that served other causes.

Another animal rights book that was a call to action was Tom Regan's *The Case for Animal Rights*. Regan argues that if "it is wrong to treat weaker human beings, especially those who are lacking in normal human intelligence, as tools or renewable resources or models or commodities, then it cannot be right, therefore, to treat other animals as tools, models and the like."[2]

In implementing their philosophy, animal rights organizations use more aggressive tactics than do the traditional humane societies. And sometimes the tactics border on terrorism.

PEOPLE FOR THE ETHICAL TREATMENT OF ANIMALS (PETA)

PETA was founded in 1980 by Alex Pacheco and Ingrid Newkirk. At the time, Pacheco was a student who had taken a course in bioethics taught by Peter Singer. Newkirk was an animal disease control officer in Washington, D.C. Starting with eighteen members, PETA quickly grew; by 1983, it claimed a membership of 12,000. Equally important, PETA's income was in the millions. The organization now has more than 250,000 members and a multimillion-dollar budget.

PETA's rather meteoric rise in strength, funding, and influence can be attributed to superior organization and dedicated membership. Although some of its philosophy is difficult for the average person to understand, especially the concepts of specieism and racism as applied to animals, the organization continues to attract recruits.

In an interview, Ingrid Newkirk stated her animal rights philosophy in no uncertain terms. She announced that human beings do not have the "right to life." In a parody of Gertrude Stein, the American author whose famous line "A rose is a rose is a rose" has often been quoted, Newkirk said, "A rat is a pig is a dog is a boy."[3]

In a 1983 *Washington Post* interview, Newkirk stated, "Six million Jews died in concentration camps, but six billion chickens will die this year in slaughterhouses." She added that animal liberationists consider meat eating "primitive, barbaric and arrogant." Pet ownership, according to Newkirk, is fascism.

PETA has achieved what it considers major victories in the crusade to liberate animals. Early on, it exposed the United States Department of Defense's planned experiments on gunshot wounds involving the use of cats and dogs. In the experiments, the animals would be shot with bullets for the purpose of studying tissue damage. However, the investigation by PETA agents and their public reports eventually forced Caspar Weinberger, then secretary of defense, to cancel the experiments.

PETA scored what animal rights activists believed to be another major victory for animal liberation when Alex Pacheco exposed the alleged neglect and inhumane treatment of monkeys. In 1981, Edward Taub, a psychologist, was conducting research at the Institute for Behavioral Research in Silver Spring, Maryland. The research involved tests to show how numbness in an arm or leg could impair its use. Taub severed the sensory nerves in one arm of experimental monkeys, a procedure known as *deafferentation*.

Pacheco posed as a college student interested in research. Under this cover, he obtained a position as an intern in the Institute for Behavioral Research, where he monitored Taub's research procedures and the treatment of the monkeys.

While on the night shift, Pacheco and another member of PETA took a photo of a monkey named Domitian (apparently named after the Roman emperor who ruled during A.D. 81–96). The photo was supposed to show the monkey's suffering while undergoing an experiment. Pacheco and his associate took Domitian out of his cage and restrained his arms and legs with straps attached to a chairlike apparatus. The photo was snapped before Domitian relaxed in the chair as he usually did before an experiment.

The restraining apparatus used by Pacheco to take his staged photo was one used by Dr. Taub for a one-hour period only. But it was never used in the way Pacheco used it for the photo. In experiments using this equipment—simulating human spinal cord injuries—a monkey was seated on a Plexiglas board with arms and legs held motionless. In this type of restraint, precise measurements of sensation loss could be made on a nerve-shattered arm or leg.

Pacheco also took photos of what were supposed to be conditions of neglect and poor sanitation in Dr. Taub's laboratory. Pacheco's evidence was enough for the police to raid Taub's laboratory. Taub was arrested and charged with 119 counts of cruelty to animals. One of the charges against him was that he failed to provide veterinary care for six monkeys; specifically, no bandages were placed on the nerve-severed arms and legs of the monkeys.

Seven veterinarians who testified at Taub's trial on the need for such bandaging failed to agree. But two other veterinarians—who were not familiar with the kind of injuries received by the monkeys—thought Taub was negligent in not bandaging them. The court agreed with these two veterinarians and found Taub guilty of cruelty to animals.

Pacheco, when questioned at the trial of Taub, admitted that when Dr. Taub was away on vacation, he—Pacheco—allowed conditions in the laboratory to go downhill and become unsanitary. He then took the photo of the deplorable conditions.[4]

Taub's arrest was the first time any researcher had been legally called to account for cruelty to animals. Eventually, the 119 charges brought against him were reduced to a single charge: failure to provide veterinary care for the monkeys as mandated in the Animal Welfare Act. But his conviction on this charge was overturned. He later went to the University of Alabama, where he applied the important information learned from the Silver Spring monkeys (as they became known) to human stroke victims.

Pacheco opened a Pandora's box of evils when he reported the alleged cruelty to animals at the Institute of Behavioral Research (IBR). Following the raid on the laboratory, the IBR wanted to transfer the monkeys to the National Institutes of Health, the agency that had approved Dr. Taub's research project. But the NIH refused to take the monkeys, stating that it had no projects, ongoing or contemplated, that could use them.

PETA wanted possession of the monkeys. After the raid, the police placed them in the care of three PETA members. They drove the monkeys to Florida in a truck. Later, when the court turned over the monkeys to the Institute for Behavioral Research, they were not in good condition. Their white blood cell counts were elevated, which indicated the primates were under severe stress; in addition, they showed signs of depression and withdrawal.

PETA and some other animal rights groups, among them the International Primate Protection League, sought custody of the monkeys. But some scientific organizations called for the completion of Dr. Taub's research since, in their opinion, it was important. They were also concerned that a precedent might be set. If a court allowed animal rights groups to bring suit over the disposition of the Silver Spring monkeys, then animal rights groups had legal standing and could sue over the use of animals in any research. This would lead to a situation that could have drastic effects on biomedical research.

Since neither the Institute for Behavioral Research nor the NIH wanted the Silver Spring monkeys, they were kept in limbo, generating bad publicity for both organizations. But something had to be done about the monkeys, and the story of their plight eventually reached Congress. Several hundred members appealed to the NIH for the transfer of the monkeys to a primate sanctuary; the NIH rejected the request. Instead of going to a sanctuary, the monkeys were hauled to the Delta Regional Primate Research Center in Covington, Louisiana. However, five monkeys that had not been operated on in Taub's laboratory were sent to the San Diego Zoo. A female monkey named Sarah, used as a control for Taub's experiments, was kept by the NIH for breeding purposes at the Delta Primate Center. Researchers there found that Sarah's ovaries had been removed, thus making her useless for breeding.

Exposure of the conditions in Taub's laboratory was regarded as a major victory by the animal rights movement. It was a black mark for biomedical research, but it was an isolated case, not an everyday occurrence in research laboratories.

In 1991, Supreme Court Justice Anthony M. Kennedy barred the NIH from killing two Silver Spring monkeys in the Delta Primate Center. The two monkeys, Allan and Titus, had been used in brain experiments under what was called "terminal anesthesia." That is, they would die after the experiments.

Justice Kennedy acted on a petition presented by PETA and other animal rights groups. The petition was an attempt to block the killing of Allan and Titus. After review, the Supreme Court overturned Justice Kennedy's order and denied the petition.

Consequently, Titus was put to sleep. But Allan was first used in a four-hour experiment that measured signals to his brain. When this study was completed, Allan died without coming out of the anesthesia. The information obtained from the experiment with Allan has been important to spinal cord research and the study of strokes.

In a 1991 mailing, which it entitled *National Referendum*, PETA stated, "Six to eight million animals will die every month in our nation's commercial, military, and federally funded university laboratories." It reaffirmed its efforts to eliminate the use of animals for product testing and stop the dissecting of animals in schools and universities.

ANIMAL LIBERATION FRONT (ALF) ⸺

ALF is an international animal rights organization with a direct action approach to the liberation of animals. It is believed that an ALF cell, or unit, was created or imported into the United States in the early 1980s. Both the FBI and Scotland Yard have labeled ALF as a terrorist organization. ALF has expanded its activities quickly, mainly because its organization and tactics had been tested in England.

ALF came to the public's notice when members broke into research laboratories, damaged equipment, destroyed records, and stole research animals. ALF claimed credit for break-ins at Howard University's Medical School and the United States Naval Research Institute located in a suburb of Washington, D.C.

ALF STRIKES AGAIN! This slogan is written on the walls of laboratories vandalized by this terrorist organization. ALF's destructive activities have resulted in higher costs for biomedical research at some colleges and universities. More than a hundred medical schools were included in a survey made by the Association of American Medical Colleges. Seventy-six reported losing more than 30,000 working hours because of break-ins, vandalism, and destruction of research records. The medical schools reported over 3,000 incidents involving faculty or staff, including harassment, bomb scares, threats of bodily harm, and even death threats.

ALF has more or less abandoned its avowed interest in eliminating inhumane treatment of animals in research laboratories. In a note left behind in an October 1986 raid on a University of Oregon laboratory, ALF agents proclaimed: "We openly concede we found few instances of noncompliance with guidelines of the Federal Animal Welfare Act governing humane care and treatment of animals."

But ALF's new approach is one of destruction instead of exposure of cruelty to animals. Breaking valuable equipment, destroying or stealing research records, releasing laboratory animals, and committing other acts of

94

vandalism—not to mention threatening researchers—are the tactics employed by this terrorist organization.

In keeping with this approach, ALF agents destroyed a $10,000 microscope in a raid on a laboratory at the University of Oregon. In the note left behind, the ALF agents bragged that the microscope had been "destroyed in about ten seconds with a steel wrecking bar purchased for less than five dollars." The note went on to say that any monetary damage they could do represents "money unavailable for the purchase, mutilation and slaughter of living animals."

Six months after the University of Oregon break-in, ALF agents set fire to an animal diagnostic laboratory being built at the University of California at Davis. The fire caused more than $4 million in damages. The California Attorney General's Office called ALF one of California's most dangerous organizations. Later, the FBI added ALF to its list of domestic terrorist organizations.

So far, with one exception, ALF agents have managed to avoid capture and arrest. The exception was Roger Troen, an agent who was involved in the University of Oregon laboratory raid. He was arrested, tried, and convicted of theft and burglary. PETA went to his rescue, paying $27,000 of his legal fees; the animal rights groups also paid his fine of $34,000.

ALF is very efficient in its plans and tactics. In 1989, its agents broke into a laboratory at the University of Arizona and made off with 11,000 experimental mice and rats. In addition to the theft of the rodents, the agents set off a bomb that damaged two buildings, causing an estimated $250,000 in damages.

In January 1990, ALF agents forced their way into the office of Adrian R. Morrison, a researcher at the University of Pennsylvania investigating patterns and effects of sleep on animals. The ALF agents stole films, videotapes, slides, and computer disks. They left behind their calling card: ALF—FIRST STRIKE! Morrison later received a telephone call in which the caller warned him that the break-in was a "gentle warning."

The ALF struck again in February of 1992 with a raid on two research facilities at Michigan State University in East Lansing. One facility was set on fire, which destroyed more than thirty years of animal science research. Equipment and property valued at more than $75,000 were also destroyed, according to the chairman of the university's animal science department. The raid was aimed at the work of Richard J. Aulerich, an animal science professor who had been conducting research on toxins and their effects on animals. His research involved feeding food containing toxic material to mink. Mink are very susceptible to toxic chemicals, such as PCB, found in contaminated fish. Professor Aulerich's research would have benefited both humans and animals.

Members of the ALF broke into Professor Aulerich's office, rifled the files, and started a fire that gutted the office. Smoke from the fire damaged two other offices, a reception area, and a conference room. The mink cages were opened, but the mink were not removed. The ALF agents spray-painted their message on the walls: AULERICH TORTURES MINKS and FUR IS MURDER.

The seriousness of the research laboratory break-ins and the damage caused by ALF agents have prompted Congress to consider some "research protection" bills. One would make it a felony to break into any research facility operating under the provisions of the Animal Welfare Act. Another would offer protection to federally funded health research facilities and primate centers. In the case of the felony bill, the Department of Agriculture would be the enforcement agency. The bill that offers protection to the health research facilities and primate centers would be enforced by the FBI. However, opinion is divided over making laboratory break-ins and vandalism federal crimes. But James Mason, a deputy assistant secretary in the Department of Health and Human Services, warned: "The people who broke into the lab [Morrison's] are terrorists. The nation must not tolerate this kind of criminal activity."

ANIMAL WELFARE INSTITUTE (AWI)

The Animal Welfare Institute, a moderate animal protection organization, is based in Washington, D.C. Its stated purpose is to "reduce the sum total of pain and fear inflicted on animals by man." The organization is involved in a broad range of activities aimed at reducing cruelty to animals. It offers numerous books, pamphlets, and articles on humane education, wildlife conservation, trapping, attitudes toward animals, and the use of animals for research.

The AWI is active in the area of animal research. It is concerned with the humane treatment of laboratory animals, proper nutrition, housing, and development of alternatives to animal testing and research. Agents of the AWI monitor animal experimentation by research facilities to ensure that they adhere to Animal Welfare Act standards.

An officer of the AWI served on a National Resource Committee that recommended that research facilities receiving public funds reduce the number of vertebrates used in experiments and consider the use of alternatives. Christine Stevens, a founder of the Animal Welfare Institute, did not sign the committee's report. She complained that the NRC refused to acknowledge the widespread problem of the unnecessary suffering that has been inflicted on laboratory animals. Nothing in the NRC report, according to Stevens, "even hinted at the long drawn-out pain and suffering undergone by many laboratory animals."

AMERICAN ANTIVIVISECTION SOCIETY (AAVS)

The American Antivivisection Society, located in Jenkintown, Pennsylvania, defines vivisection as the "cutting, burning, freezing, poisoning, crushing, starving, internally or externally mutilating, shocking or subjecting to every conceivable kind of stress—any animal that can be handled in a laboratory." With this lengthy definition, the AAVS has stretched the original definition of vivisection, cutting into the body, to one that includes any action against or experiment on an animal.

Vivisection continues, according to the AAVS, because of grants from public and private agencies such as the National Institutes of Health on the public side and the Ford and Rockefeller foundations in the private sector. The AAVS charges that much of the biomedical research using animals is worthless in terms of relevancy to human beings.

The AAVS offers brochures, books, audiovisual aids, and other material dealing with vivisection and suffering of laboratory animals. It distributes buttons that state, ANIMAL EXPERIMENTS ARE CRUEL: STOP THEM. An AAVS poster states: HELP STOP VIVISECTION.

The AAVS, like the Animal Welfare Institute, does not engage in or condone violence or vandalism in spreading its message. Instead, it publishes articles and reports in a monthly publication, *The AV Magazine.*

AMERICAN HUMANE ASSOCIATION (AHA)

The AHA, a federation of American humane societies, was founded in the latter part of the nineteenth century. Its main purpose then was to campaign for the protection of the diminishing bison and livestock being shipped on railroads. In the twentieth century, the AHA has broadened its scope of activities on behalf of animals, including addressing the issue of animals in research.

This older animal protection organization offers an educational program that covers various areas in which animals are exploited or abused. And like other moderate organizations, the AHA does not condone violence or vandalism in efforts to protect animals from abuse and misuse. It maintains a staff of investigators who look into situations involving animal abuse, from research to use of animals in films and television.

HUMANE SOCIETY OF THE UNITED STATES (HSUS)

The HSUS is another federation of humane societies in the United States, with functions similar to those of the AHA. It maintains an educational division, a group of investigators, and a cadre of legislative experts.

On the matter of the use of animals in research, a HSUS fact sheet states, "Although animal research may have scientific merit in some cases, it is often painful and stressful to animals; costly; time-consuming; and unlikely to improve human health." The HSUS believes that the evaluation of animal research projects should address the following questions:

> Can the use of animals in an experiment be replaced by nonanimal methods that would yield comparable or superior results? If not, can the proposed number of animals for use in an experiment be reduced to a minimum without compromising results?
> Can the proposed procedures be refined so that any pain, suffering, or deprivation experienced by the animals be minimized without compromising results?

With these questions, the HSUS emphasizes the three R's of a more humane approach to animal experimentation:

99

that is, *replacement* by other methods or alternatives, *reduction* in the number of animals used per experiment, and *refinement* of experiment procedures. Many researchers are using this approach in their experiments or studies.

AMERICAN SPCA (ASPCA)

Another leading moderate animal welfare organization is the American SPCA, founded in New York City by the humanitarian Henry Bergh in 1866. The ASPCA does not demand the total abolition of animal research, but it does take the position that animal experimentation should be allowed only when there is no known or feasible alternative. Even then, any experiment should be expected to produce new and substantive information; there should be no repetitive experiments. Furthermore, experiments should be designed to use the minimum number of the most suitable species. The animals should be maintained in a sanitary environment and treated humanely during and after an experiment. All efforts should be made to reduce pain and suffering.

This humane society—the first in the United States—does not approve of violence or terrorism in pursuing its policy of eliminating cruelty to animals. It has an extensive education program, including a videotape, "A Question of Respect," which explores the subject of animal research. The tape stresses the need to develop alternatives and advocates a balance between the rights of animals and the requirements of ethical scientific research.

The foregoing animal rights and welfare organizations might be considered the leaders in the animal rights movement since they receive the most public attention. However, many more organizations are involved in the crusade to reduce cruelty to animals, both in research and in other areas of animal exploitation. They include many

SPCAs, such as the Massachusetts SPCA and the Pennsylvania SPCA, two older and moderate animal welfare organizations; newer groups composed of physicians, veterinarians, and psychologists; and smaller but militant animal rights groups.

Their positions range from reforms in the use of animals in research to the abolition of animal research to the liberation of animals from all forms of exploitation. While these organizations do not receive the notice or headlines that PETA, ALF, or the other leading animal rights groups do, they are active in the movement. Here are some of them.

MEDICAL RESEARCH MODERNIZATION COMMITTEE (MRMC)

The MRMC organization suggests in a report, "A Critical Look at Animal Research," that the use of animals in research continues for several reasons. One is that in the academic world, scientists must "publish or perish." Animal research, according to the MRMC, provides a route to the publication of articles and books. It is easy, states the MRMC, to change a few variables in an experiment and come up with new or interesting results suitable for publication. Another reason for the continued use of animals in research is that experiments on animals can be completed sooner than those on human beings because of the shorter life spans of laboratory animals.

More scientists, according to the MRMC report, have been trained in the use of animals for research. It is difficult for them to switch to alternatives such as tissue cultures and computer simulations. Also, the report continues, scientists can prove nearly anything with animals. That is, by using various animal species, researchers can confirm almost any theory they select. Researchers deny these charges.

PHYSICIANS COMMITTEE FOR RESPONSIBLE MEDICINE (PCRM)

The PCRM is a Washington, D.C., based organization that lists physicians, scientists, and medical students among its members. Its approach to the animals in research issue is one of promoting the development and use of alternatives. Members are active in various fields of medicine and science; one member, Dr. Ruy Tchao, developed an alternative to the controversial Draize test. The PCRM advocates a balance between the rights of animals and the requirements of ethical scientific research.

ASSOCIATION OF VETERINARIANS FOR ANIMAL RIGHTS (AVAR)

In a position paper, the AVAR stated that the "issue is highly complex partly because of the prevailing perception that the use of nonhuman animals in research is the key to improving our health and increasing our longevity and comfort."

While the AVAR recognizes that there are some benefits from using animals in research, it does not believe that the end justifies the means. It calls for an end to the dependence on animals for research, especially when such research "leads to their harm." This organization of veterinarians calls for more legislation to control and monitor all animal experiments.

The AVAR recommends the creation of a national or international data base of information for researchers to eliminate duplication of experiments. While making its demands and recommendations, the AVAR recognizes that the use of animals in research will continue "into the foreseeable future." It does not advocate violence or terrorism.

* * *

Researchers in Canada have also had their share of animal rights accusations, charges, and obstructive tactics. Especially singled out by the animal rights activists is the University of Toronto, which activists claim is the largest user of experimental animals in Canada. They charge the university's medical science, dentistry, zoology, and psychology departments with the use of more than 90,000 animals annually in research projects.

Targeted by the animal rights activists were experiments performed in the university's dentistry department. They charged that cats from local pounds, along with some monkeys, were used in painful experiments. The purpose of the experiments was to chart the pathways in the brain that are responsible for the perceptions of pain. It was alleged that dentistry researchers did not use any anesthesia or analgesics. One University of Toronto alumnus had this to say about these experiments: "The pain we undergo voluntarily at the dentist is acceptable; the incomprehensible pain and helpless terror suffered by an animal at the hands of 'dental scientists' is not."

When the animal rights advocates raised the issue of the use of animals in research to a national controversy in the 1970s and 1980s, they caught the scientific community more or less flat-footed. Researchers were unprepared for the intensity of the assault by the animal rights movement. But they have recovered and defend their research with rational arguments and scientific facts.

"The current animal rights movement threatens the future of health science far more than many physicians recognize." This statement appeared in an article in *The New England Journal of Medicine*.[5] The authors went on to say that the "movement is no fringe group of fanatics who cannot have a serious effect on the real world." The article pointed out that by impugning the motives of researchers (the need to publish, the competition for grant money, and so on) and giving an inaccurate picture of the conditions under which most animal experiments are

103

performed, the leaders of the movement have won the support of "well-intentioned but misguided followers."

David T. Hardy, an attorney in the Washington Legal Foundation, also had something to say about the animal rights movement. In his booklet, *America's New Extremists: What You Need to Know about the Animal Rights Movement*, he wrote, "Animal rights activists might be regarded as harmless eccentrics, were it not for the fact that others are willing to take them quite seriously and put them into action, often violent action."[6]

Finally, Susan Sperking, a cultural anthropologist and the author of *Animal Liberators: Research and Morality*, argues that animal rights activists "relate to animals as people." They anthropomorphize animals; that is, they attribute human traits and motivations to animals. But, according to Sperking, pets are the only animals most animal rights activists come into contact with on a daily basis.

Regardless of how animal rights advocates are viewed, collectively they are a strong and influential force in the animal protection field. Scientists are concerned about the growing strength of the animal rights movement. They are worried about the future of their research, important for both human beings and animals. They resent the charges made by the animal rights activists and antivivisectionists. They realize they cannot retreat or ignore the controversy. And so they have answered the charges of the animal rights advocates and antivivisectionists with refinements of experiments, reduction in the use of animals, and a continuous search for alternatives to the use of animals in research.

ALTERNATIVES TO THE
USE OF ANIMALS

A number of alternatives to the use of animals in research, product testing, and education have been developed since the rise of the animal rights movement. However, their availability does not mean an immediate end to the use of animals; there are some drawbacks in their general application to biomedical research and product testing.

What is an alternative? A standard definition is "one of two or more things that may be chosen." In the research field it amounts to animal versus nonanimal use. But the word has different meanings in the animals in research controversy. For some people, it means a technique or method that totally replaces animals in research or product testing, such as a substitute for the controversial LD/50 test. Another meaning of alternative as applied to biomedical research or testing is a technique that reduces the need for animals.

A number of public and private research centers are at work in developing alternatives. A leader in this important field is the Center for Alternatives to Animal Testing (CAAT) at Johns Hopkins University in Baltimore, Maryland. This center—the largest of its kind in the world—fosters and funds research aimed at developing in vitro and other techniques not using whole animals. (*Whole animal* is a term used in research. It differentiates between a whole live or dead animal and its organs or parts as used in research or product testing.)

The center has managed to avoid taking sides in the animals in research controversy. Its director, Alan M. Goldberg, puts it this way: "For a long time CAAT stayed out of the politics and focused on science and testing. However, we have not been allowed to be silent. We have become vocal about the appropriate use of animals in testing and research, and try to provide factual information on the status and reality of alternatives."[1]

Some alternatives now use cell and tissue cultures in vitro; microorganisms and other species believed to have limited or no feeling for pain or suffering, such as invertebrates like protozoa; computer models that can provide answers or guidance in research procedures or techniques; fewer animals per experiment or study; fewer techniques that cause pain and discomfort.

A number of manufacturers are developing alternatives for testing the safety of their products. For instance, Colgate-Palmolive, one of the major corporations that reduced its use of animals as a result of the actions and pressures of PETA and other animal rights organizations, has developed an alternative known as the chorioallantoic membrane assay, or CAM, and uses fetal membrane material. The test is used to prescreen new formulas and ingredients for safety. According to Colgate-Palmolive, the corporation research facility's use of animals for experiments and testing products has been reduced by as much as 90 percent.

Another large corporation, Hoffman-LaRoche, a pharmaceutical manufacturer in New Jersey, has also reduced its use of animals by more than 60 percent. It has done so by computer-assisted modeling, a technique that allows researchers to see the shape and structure of a chemical or substance in a three-dimensional image on a computer screen. However, computer modeling may not totally replace the use of animals; rather, it fits into the reduction and refinement category of animal research.

Researchers using in vitro tests obtain specific cells— human or animal—depending on the specific study or experiment. In product testing, a chemical or substance is applied to the cells and monitored for reactions or responses. There are some disadvantages to cell culture. One is that some cells change character when cultured; another is that the supply of specific cells may be limited from time to time.

In vitro methodology, while promising to replace, re- duce, and refine animal experiments, has not progressed as rapidly as expected because of some difficulties and technicalities. One is that federal regulations require spe- cific tests of a chemical or product before it can be ap- proved for release to the public. For example, the United States Environmental Protection Agency (EPA) can re- quire toxicology testing under two of its statutes, the Fed- eral Insecticide, Fungicide and Rodenticide Act and the Toxic Substance Act.

The EPA evaluates chemicals and other potentially harmful substances for their toxicity as shown by short- and long-term animal exposure tests, that is, acute and chronic toxicity tests, on animals. The EPA considers ani- mal tests to be critical elements in toxicity evaluations.

Another barrier to progress in the use of in vitro and other alternatives is that manufacturers are still fearful of lawsuits. Should a consumer or user of a product have an adverse reaction to a product or substance that has been tested on alternatives, rather than by the standard animal tests, a lawsuit might easily go against a manufac- turer. Thus there is resistance to the use of alternatives among some manufacturers. Another factor in the reluc- tant use of alternatives by some manufacturers is that they are new and have not been time-tested as have the standard animal tests. Equally important, in vitro and other nonanimal methods need to be standardized and validated.

The development of cell culture tests is proceeding slowly because of certain considerations. One is that a single cell in culture cannot produce exactly the same responses or interactions that take place in all other cells in a human or animal body. The reactions and responses in cells in vitro may not always be exact copies of the ones that actually occur in the body.

THE VALIDATION OF ALTERNATIVES _____

The validation of in vitro tests and other nonanimal methods is crucial for their acceptance by industry and federal regulatory agencies. Progress in validating nonanimal tests or methods has been slow, a major impediment being the lack of coordination among testing laboratories.

There are some other problems, one of which concerns the Ames test developed by Dr. Bruce Ames. This test employs bacterial cultures as an alternative to the use of animals in identifying cancer-causing agents in a chemical or substance. The test picks out carcinogens by their ability to produce mutations in a special strain of *Salmonella* bacteria. But this test has what some critics call a weakness—a chemical that passes the Ames test could, in human beings, be metabolized into a carcinogen or could cause the formation of cancer-causing tumors.

For an alternative test to be validated, it must undergo two major steps or stages: (1) the test must be standardized—it must be described or defined in a form that can be duplicated by other researchers in other laboratories; (2) the laboratory that develops the alternative test or method must perform what is known as a "blind study." The purpose of this study is to make sure there are no built-in irregularities in the test results.

108

After an alternative has passed through these stages, it is subjected to duplication in different laboratories. (This procedure is known as macrovalidation.) Once an in vitro or other alternative test has passed through these important stages, a nucleus of a data base has been established. This data base can be used to evaluate the accuracy and reliability of an alternative test or technique.

Since alternative tests are relatively new and not widely used at the present time, they have not provided a substantial backlog of data, nor is their data base comparable to that accumulated by animal tests over many years. Animal tests and experiments have offered a method of assessing and quantifying the risks in a chemical or other substance. Although condemned by animal rights advocates and antivivisectionists, animal testing has undoubtedly protected the public from the hazards of toxic chemicals and substances, such as food additives and pesticides.

RISK ASSESSMENT

What is the risk involved in the use of a cosmetic? Of a detergent? Of consumption of a certain food with various additives? The answers lie in the evaluation of a chemical or substance on a short- or long-term exposure basis. Information obtained from in vitro and other studies and tests involving animals is used to evaluate the risk in consuming or using food or products containing potentially harmful chemicals or substances. Some critics say that no single in vitro test has yet reached the stage where it is unconditionally validated. They believe that a battery of tests will be required for risk evaluation for any given chemical or substance.

Researchers at the Center for Alternatives to Animal Testing believe that results of the search for and development of new alternatives will be a "tier system of testing." That is, it will consist of a series, or rows, of tests. In a tier system, chemicals and products will be tested first by computer simulations, then by a nonanimal test such as the Ames test. Ultimately, by passing through these tiers or stages, only safe products or substances will reach the final tier: testing on animals. The tier system is expected to reduce the number of animals required for testing a specific product.

The end of animal testing is some distance away. The National Research Council is of the opinion that alternatives will never completely replace use of animals in product testing and certainly not in biomedical and behavioral research. The NRC also believes that to abandon the use of animals in biomedical research would be counterproductive because important health benefits to both human beings and animals would be lost. Also, the total abandonment of the use of animals in biomedical research could lead to unethical research and more testing on human beings than is being performed at the present time.[2] (As an example, some AIDS patients are more or less human "guinea pigs" since they are taking unproven drugs as a last resort because of desperation.)

ALTERNATIVES TO ANIMALS IN BIOMEDICAL RESEARCH

Despite the efforts of researchers to practice the three R's of humane research, animal rights advocates and antivivisectionists clamor for the abolition of the use of animals in biomedical and behavioral research. Some scientists believe that people do not understand or appreciate the importance of both types of research. Nor do they seem to realize, according to researchers, that animals are indispensable in biomedical and behavioral research. Certain experiments and studies cannot be performed or conducted with in vitro or other nonanimal techniques. Alternatives are not, as yet, total substitutes for use of animals in biomedical and behavioral research, research that yields benefits for both human beings and animals.

There is no question that having substitutes for animals in biomedical and behavioral research is highly desirable. Progress has been made in developing and using some alternatives, although scientists say there are no realistic substitutes for living organisms.

Animals are still a valuable part of research into disease. Rhesus monkeys may play an important role in producing data on Parkinson's disease, a neurological disorder that destroys brain cells and afflicts older persons with palsy (loss of feeling or control of movement of some part of the body, such as head, hands, and feet) and muscle rigidity. The experimental monkeys are given a drug that destroys specific cells in the same area of the brain affected by Parkinson's disease, and the monkeys exhibit all of the symptoms seen in human patients afflicted with it. The monkeys used in the Parkinson's disease research responded well to levodopa, a drug now used to treat the disease in humans. So far, no alternatives have been developed to take the place of animals in this field of biomedical research.

Tissue cultures are now being used as alternatives in some areas of biomedical research. Certain human and animal tissues continue to live after having been removed from the original organism, but they must be maintained in a culture dish. Using this technique, a wide range of in vitro methods have been developed, including subcellular refraction, use of tissue biopsies, and study of tissue slices.

Two types of tissue culture are in use: cell culture and organ culture. In cell culture, the cells are kept under conditions that allow them to survive and multiply. Researchers obtain cells for culturing from several sources—autopsies, fetuses, human and animal placenta, and animals that have been humanely destroyed.

Since the abortion issue is still very controversial, the

use of human aborted fetuses for research has been challenged. At the present time, only fetuses from tubular pregnancies and miscarriages may be used for research. In the spring of 1992, Congress passed a bill that would permit the use of aborted fetuses. President Bush said he would veto the bill unless it limited the use of human fetuses to miscarriages and tubular pregnancies. Researchers say these sources are not satisfactory, since such fetuses may be infected or otherwise unsuitable for research in such areas as Parkinson's and Alzheimer's diseases.

The approach to organ culture is different. Here the emphasis is on preserving the tissue structure and function of an organ such as a kidney or liver. Organ culture is a short-term technique, one that usually requires the sacrifice of an animal after an organ culture is established. A main advantage of organ culture is that a number of cultures can be established from a single donor animal.

There are some advantages in using in vitro systems as opposed to whole animals. One is the greater sensitivity of an in vitro technique. Another is that the experimental conditions of an in vitro experiment are more easily controlled than those of an animal experiment. Still another is the greater speed at which an in vitro experiment can be performed. Important, too, is the relatively lower cost of in vitro techniques compared to most animal experiments. But in vitro techniques may have some limitations, for example, a lack of neurological, hormonal, and immunological controls.[3]

Computer modeling is another alternative that can be used in some forms of biomedical research. This technique can provide mathematical models of human systems such as the circulatory and central nervous systems. It is possible to design mathematical and computer-assisted models of biochemical processes, but there are some limitations to this alternative. For one thing, the development of such models depends largely on the amount and quality of the data used in making them. Furthermore, researchers may include data obtained from whole animal studies or experiments. Another point is that an animal study may be needed for validating a computer model.

In vitro techniques are being used to obtain a new understanding of the action of the HIV (the virus that causes AIDS) on cells. In another research area, tissue cultures are being used to investigate certain aspects of diabetes, cancer, glaucoma, cystic fibrosis, muscular dystrophy, and certain other diseases.

A new and potentially controversial alternative is the use of transgenic animals. A transgenic animal is one that has new genes put into place by the microinjection of purified DNA. The insertion is made into the pronucleus of a fertilized egg. This transference of genetic material (it is possible to microinject human genetic material into mice)[4] leads to its integration into the DNA chromosomes of the chosen animal. It is later transmitted as a trait that can be inherited by succeeding generations.

Where do transgenic animals fit into the alternative category? After all, a transgenic animal is still an animal. Researchers using transgenic animals can be accused of furthering the use of animals in biomedical research, and, more than that, there are ethical considerations in "creating" such creatures.

There are a number of cases in which transgenic technology, or "genetic engineering," has resulted in the creation of some unusual animal models, for example, hepatitis B transgenic mice. Investigators have shown that the "expression of hepatitis B surface antigen in transgenic mouse liver can induce a disease state that resembles chronic hepatitis."[5] Chimpanzees have been the main models for hepatitis studies, but transgenic mice can now replace these costly and endangered animals.

Transgenic mice can be used as models in certain HIV studies. Mice, like chimpanzees and other animals, do not develop AIDS. This would be another area of biomedical research in which study of transgenic rodents could reduce dependence on the use of larger and rarer species.

Another important biomedical research area in which transgenic animals can be used is in investigations on Alzheimer's disease. Prior to the creation of transgenic animals, only a few animals, such as the chimpanzee and rhesus monkey, were involved in studies on Alzheimer's disease. Alzheimer's-like symptoms have been observed in old primates, but rodents have not displayed any evidence of this disease. However, researchers have demonstrated that by inserting a portion of an amyloid precursor (APP) (found in Alzheimer's disease) into transgenic mice, Alzheimer's-like symptoms occur.

The use of transgenic mice and rats can reduce the use of larger animals. But is it a true alternative? All these "new" animals do is shift the emphasis of certain animal use in biomedical research from larger animals to smaller ones. Use of transgenic rodents as an alternative is questionable as far as getting approval from animal rights advocates and antivivisectionists, especially since they are actively campaigning to obtain protection for mice, rats, and rabbits.

ALTERNATIVES TO THE USE OF ANIMALS IN EDUCATION _____

As in biomedical research and animal testing, there is a demand for the use of alternatives in schools, colleges, and universities. The National Association of Biology Teachers (NABT) supports the use of alternatives in the classroom whenever feasible. According to the NABT, alternatives must "satisfy the objectives of teaching scientific methodology and fundamental biology concepts."[6] The NABT emphasizes that the continued but modified use of living animals cannot be avoided in some areas of biology instruction and learning. This would include experiments on invertebrates and behavioral studies on vertebrates. Regardless of how animals will be used in the classroom or biology laboratory, the NABT recommends their responsible use, with special attention to their humane treatment and care.

There is a wide range of alternatives for high school and college use. They include X rays of animal and human anatomy and systems; heart imaging; computer models; films and film strips; audiovisual aids; computed tomography (CT) scans; magnetic resonance imaging; pyelograms of kidneys; and take-apart animal and human models. Medical and veterinary students have special alternatives, such as videotapes, manual skills simulators, clinical problem solving kits, and computer simulations.

Will alternatives ultimately replace animals in biomedical and behavioral research product testing and education as antivivisectionists and animal rights activists say they should?

The Committee on the Use of Laboratory Animals in Biomedical and Behavioral Research was appointed by the National Research Council in 1985. It was composed of representatives of a number of colleges and universities, a pharmaceutical manufacturer, a state health department, a cancer research center, and a humane society. No animal rights activist was appointed to the committee; the lone animal protection representative was Christine Stevens of the Animal Welfare Institute.

After a long study, the committee published its findings and conclusions. Among them were the following:

In many instances, a specific animal procedure or experiment is the best or only system for conducting research on a particular biological process. However, alternative methods may allow researchers to reduce the number of animals used in an experiment or a study. Some nonanimal models can replace animals in certain research areas. And some alternatives can refine experimental procedures so as to minimize pain and suffering (the three R's of humane research).

The committee recommended that researchers consider alternatives *before* using animals in an experiment or study, and that data bases be further developed and made available to researchers seeking appropriate experimental alternatives.

The tactics of the animal rights groups are not acceptable to everyone. Nevertheless, they have achieved a major victory: They took the issue of the use of animals in research out of the laboratories and into the open. The welfare of laboratory animals has improved through the efforts of both the animal rights movement and the scientific community. More manufacturers have stopped using animals to test their products or are using fewer animals for that purpose. The three *R*'s are now the condition under which biomedical research is being conducted. High school, university, and medical and veterinary students are using alternatives to animal experiments. More laboratory animal protection laws are being considered by state and local legislators. And the search for more alternatives goes on.

But there are problems still to be solved. The main one involves the human element. Antagonisms, emotions, confrontations, name-calling, threats of vandalism, and violence—all of these still cast shadows over the future of scientific research.

More rational people believe that what will be needed in the years ahead are compromise, better communication, less disinformation and misinformation, and appeals to reason rather than emotion. Both sides—the animal rights movement and the scientific community—must bend, must strive to reach an accord that will benefit animals and people. There must be accountability to the public for both sides, for it is the public that funds a great deal of research and the animal rights movement. The public must understand that animals may never be totally replaced in research, but that through the consistent use of the three *R*'s of humane research, much pain and suffering can be reduced and even eliminated.

116

Source Notes

CHAPTER ONE
1. National Academy of Sciences, Research Council Report, *Use of Laboratory Animals in Biomedical and Behavioral Research* (Washington, D.C.: National Academy Press, 1988).
2. Office of Technology Assessment, *Alternatives to Animal Use in Research and Testing and Education* (Washington, D.C.: U.S. Government Printing Office, 1986).
3. John Paul Scott, *Animal Behavior* (Chicago: University of Chicago Press, 1958).

CHAPTER TWO
1. N. C. Pederson et al., "Isolation of a Lymphotropic Lentivirus from Domestic Cats with Immuno-Deficiency-Like Syndrome" *Science* 1987 235: 790–793.
2. Charles M. Balch et al., "The Vital Role of Animal Research in Advancing Cancer Diagnosis and Treatment" *Cancer Bulletin*, University of Texas, M. D.

Anderson Cancer Center, 42 (4) July–August 1990, 266–269.

3. Medical Research Modernization Committee, *A Critical Look at Animal Research* (New York: The Committee, 1990), 10.

4. American Medical Association, *Use of Animals in Biomedical Research: The Challenge and Response* (Chicago: AMA, 1989).

CHAPTER THREE

1. U.S. Senate Subcommittee on Science, Research and Technology Hearing, May 6, 1986 *Congressional Record* (Washington, D.C.: U.S. Government Printing Office, 1986), 10.

2. Humane Society of the United States, *Classical LD/50 Acute Toxicity Test* (Washington, D.C.: The Society, 1984).

CHAPTER FOUR

1. "Tactics Turn Rabid in Dissection War," *Insight* (Sept. 23, 1991), 21.

2. Warren F. Walker, "Anatomy and Dissection of the Fetal Pig," *Laboratory Exercise 5* (New York: W. H. Foreman and Company, 1988), 4.

3. American Antivivisection Society, *What Do All These Institutions Have in Common?* (Jenkintown, Pa.: The Society, 1990).

4. N. D. Barnard et al., "Use of and Alternatives to Animals in Laboratory Courses in U.S. Medical Schools" *Journal of Medical Education* 1988 63 (9) 720–722.

CHAPTER FIVE

1. Animal Welfare Act (as amended) 7 U.S.C. 2131–2157 Digest Section 2 e.

2. U.S. Department of Health and Human Services, National Institutes of Health, *Guide for the Care and Use of Laboratory Animals*, Publication No 86–23

(Washington, D.C.: U.S. Government Printing Office, 1985).
3. Canadian Council on Animal Care, *Guide to the Care and Use of Experimental Animals*, 2 vols. (Ottawa, Ontario: The Council, 1984).
4. House of Representatives Bill 1389, "To promote the dissemination of biomedical information through modern methods of science and technology and to prevent the duplication of experiments on live animals."

CHAPTER SIX
1. Peter Singer, *Animal Liberation* (New York: Random House, 1980).
2. Tom Regan, *The Case for Animal Rights* (Berkeley: University of California Press, 1983).
3. Katie McCabe, "Beyond Cruelty," reprint from *The Washingtonian* February 1990 25 (5).
4. Ibid.
5. Herbert Pardes et al., "Physicians and the Animal Rights Movement" *New England Journal of Medicine* June 6, 1991 124 (23) 1640–1643.
6. David T. Hardy, *America's New Extremists: What You Need to Know about the Animal Rights Movement* (Washington, D.C.: Washington Legal Foundation, 1990).

CHAPTER SEVEN
1. Alan M. Goldberg, Johns Hopkins Center for Alternatives to Animal Testing, Newsletter, Baltimore, Spring 1991, 4.
2. National Research Council, *Use of Laboratory Animals in Biomedical and Behavioral Research* (Washington, D.C.: National Academy Press, 1988).
3. National Research Council, *Use of Laboratory Animals in Biomedical and Behavioral Research* (Washington, D.C.: National Academy Press, 1988).

4. Jon Gordon, "Transgenic Animals as Alternatives to Animal Testing," Johns Hopkins Center for Alternatives to Animal Testing *Newsletter* Fall 1991 9 (2), 8–9.
5. Ibid.
6. National Association of Biology Teachers, *Policy Statement* (Reston, Va.: The Association, 1989).

FOR FURTHER READING

Fox, Michael Allen. *The Case for Animal Experimentation: An Evolutionary and Ethical Perspective*. Berkeley: University of California Press, 1986.

Langley, Gill, ed. *Animal Experimentation: The Consensus Changes*. New York: Chapman and Hall, 1989.

National Research Council. *The Future of Animals, Cells, Models and Systems in Research, Development and Testing*. Washington, D.C.: National Academy of Sciences Press, 1977.

Regan, Tom. *The Case for Animal Rights*. Berkeley: University of California Press, 1983.

Rowan, Andrew N. *Of Mice, Models and Men*. Albany: State University of New York Press, 1984.

Singer, Peter. *Animal Liberation*. New York: Random House, 1980.

Index

Animal and Plant Health Inspection Service (APHIS), 25, 72, 76
Animal behavior, 21
Animal experimentation. *See also* Animal rights advocates; Biomedical research; Consumer product testing
    alternatives to, 49–50, 105–16
    care guidelines, 26, 74–78, 80–83
    educational uses, 61–70, 114–16
    by government agencies, 22
    history, 7–13, 15–17
    importance of, 19–28, 41–42
    pain during, 35–36, 53–54, 75, 82–83, 103
    regulation of, 25–26
Animal Liberation, 24, 87–88
Animal Liberation Front (ALF), 57, 68, 93–97
Animal Liberators: Research and Morality, 104
Animal protection laws, 57, 71–86
Animal Rescue League, 79
Animal Research Facility Protection Act (1990), 85

Animal rights advocates. *See also* Animal Liberation Front (ALF); People for the Ethical Treatment of Animals (PETA)
    history, 8–9
    tactics, 57, 103–4, 116–17
    views of, 23, 43–44, 59–60, 64, 83–89
Animal Welfare Act, 23, 39, 48, 68, 70–72, 77, 91
Animal Welfare Insitute (AWI), 62, 64, 97
Animals, Man and Morals, 87
Animals for Research Act, 1969 (Canada), 79
Antivivisectionists, 19, 23, 44, 83–86
Association of Veterinarians for Animal Rights (AVAR), 102
Aulerich, Richard J., 96
AV Magazine, The, 98
Avon, 50, 55, 57

Behavioral research, 36–38
Bentham, Jeremy, 8, 22
Bergh, Henry, 100
Bioethics, 88
Biomedical research
    advances/

179 McCoy, J. J.
MCC
    Animals in research

19.14

	DATE DUE		
MR 28 '94			
AP 13 '94			
AP 28 '94			
Beattie			
Weir			
AR 8 T 30			
FE 21 '95			
AP 24 '95			
NO 29 '95			